The Björn Borg Story

Björn Borg
The Björn Borg Story

translated from the Swedish
by Joan Tate

Henry Regnery Company – Chicago

First published in Great Britain by
Pelham Books Ltd, London

Published in the United States in 1975 by
Henry Regnery Company
180 North Michigan Avenue, Chicago, Illinois 60601

ISBN: 0–8092–8184–8

Manufactured in Great Britain

1. Ice-hockey, tennis and homework

Like most small boys in Södertälje, I had idols in the ice-hockey team. I was nine years old and my great aim was to become a national hockey-player with the Södertälje Sports Club. That was when what I call the turning point in my life came. My father, who for many years had been one of the country's best table-tennis players and had almost played for his country in his twenties, came home with a tennis-racket he had won as a prize.

I was given the racket "to play about with", but I lived only a hundred yards or so from the park's tennis courts and my interest in tennis increased the moment my father gave me the racket. The following day, I asked one of the coaches in the Södertälje Tennis Club if there were any vacancies in the beginner class. I remember how the answer dampened my delight in my present:

"Afraid not. We have so many juniors in the club, and at the moment the beginner classes are over-subscribed."

The garage wall

But I had made up my mind to give tennis as good a chance as ice-hockey. I went home and began to hit a ball against the garage wall. I carried on with this from morning to night for three or four weeks, and as I found it almost impossible to hit the ball to start with, I played imaginary matches against the wall to keep the ball in play and sharpen my attention. I invented international matches between Sweden and the USA, and if I managed to keep the ball in play a certain number of times, Sweden won the point. If I missed, the USA did. After six weeks, I went back to the tennis club and this time was more successful.

From then on, I went to the tennis courts at seven o'clock every morning and hung around there waiting for a chance to be able to train a little more when my lesson-time was over. I refused to go home until my parents came to fetch me in the evening.

Living on the tennis court

During that summer holiday, I practically lived on the tennis courts. My interest in tennis grew every day as my basic strokes began to develop, and my obstinacy knew no limits. Many people have asked me where I acquired this persistence and I have always replied "from my parents". Before I was given my first tennis racket, I often went out on Sunday trips with them, and they nearly always arranged some sort of competition. We used to play darts, too, which the whole family enjoyed, except that I would get so angry if I lost! I made myself take part in more and more competitions; I wanted to throw over and over

5

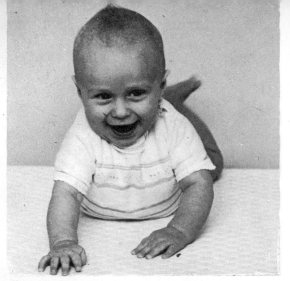

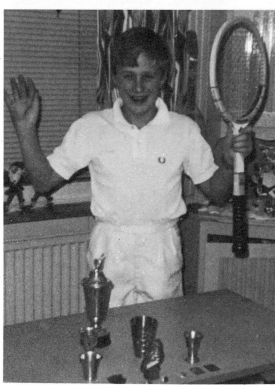

At six months old, *above left*. *Above right*, at seven years old and just starting
school. *Below left*, as an ice-hockey player. I am the one not looking
at the camera. *Bottom right*, after winning my first School Championship,
Christmas 1968

6

A great deal was written about the young tennis hopes from Södertälje during the summer of 1970. *Above left*, with my "neighbour" Leif Johansson, after winning our classes in the Båstad tournament. *Right*, after winning in the first Donald Duck Cup and waving to the photographer, with Torbjörn Fasth and Helena Anliot. *Below*, receiving the second prize in the King's Cup from Lennart Bergelin

again, and I'm sure my mother and father finally let me win! As a small boy, I was convinced I had won because of my skill, and naturally this was my parents' intention, to impress on me the importance of never giving up.

My parents have meant an enormous amount to me in my career, and I owe an equally large part in my success to my coach, Percy Rosberg.

Meeting Percy
I was ten years old when I met Percy for the first time. The Swedish Tennis Association had sent him to Södertälje to train the best juniors, which concerned first and foremost two very promising boys, Leif Johansson and Peter Åbrink. Before Percy went back to Stockholm, I too had been allowed to knock up with him for twenty minutes or so and I remember immediately appreciating Percy's method of coaching, a mixture of encouragement, criticism and praise.

Then the tournaments began. And the victories. After three years' coaching, I brought back a County medal from Sörmland by defeating Lars-Göran Nyman from Katrineholm in the final, and at twelve, I won my class in the School Tournaments.

Perhaps I should have specialised in tennis there and then, but I still preferred the combination of tennis and ice-hockey, and I also played a little football. Football was the first to be dropped, not without some regret. I was extremely interested in all sports, but tennis and ice-hockey were an easier combination than tennis and football. By the time I was fourteen, I had cut down my ice-hockey training to Wednesdays only and after an especially successful spell of tennis, including two school championships and a trip to a junior tournament in Berlin, I knew that tennis would offer the greatest rewards.

2. Full-time tennis player

A year later I had made yet another decision. I was to leave school and become a full-time tennis-player. I know that this decision came as a sensation to many people—to my school friends, most of my coaches and to tennis journalists. The news was in glaring headlines in the newspapers. But my parents and I considered there was no alternative, and with the agreement of my future employers, the Swedish Tennis Association, I left Blombacka School.

Here is a detailed account of what happened.

My first term in grade nine I managed relatively well, but tennis took up nearly all my time, and when the second term started, I felt the gap between me and my school friends growing greater and greater, until in the end it became hopeless.

Complaints from teachers

I did not keep up with my homework and my teachers began to complain. I especially remember a woman teacher who taught geography and biology, and whom I had long regarded as a typical hater of sports. She took every opportunity of revealing how little I knew, how badly I had done my homework, and when she asked me questions, I produced the consequences of her reasoning: "There's no point in your asking me questions, because I know nothing, anyhow." She was extremely angry and punished me by refusing permission for time off.

However, other teachers showed greater understanding for my tennis training, my matches, tournaments and tennis trips, and gave me a great deal of time off. Sometimes I was allowed to leave school in the middle of lessons, to be able to practise and play in important matches. Then the decision was made, or rather what my parents and I had hoped would be a decision. We arranged a meeting with my class-teacher and put our proposal to him. But he did not wish to take the responsibility of my leaving school.

I was going to leave school

This attitude did not influence me in the slightest. I *was* going to leave school and I *had* decided. A month or two later I was summoned to the Headmaster. He largely repeated what my class-teacher had said: "You can't simply leave. You just can't. You have to finish grade nine."

I was in despair over this last comment, as I knew my marks would get worse and worse, so it would be quite meaningless simply to go on sitting there between eight o'clock and three, wasting my time. Stubbornness saved me. I wouldn't give up and kept on going to see the Headmaster, several times a week, until finally he surrendered.

"Perhaps we can arrange it, but first we must meet a number of authorities and talk to them."

So we met, my parents, my class-teacher, the Headmaster and I, and we talked about school and tennis for several hours. It was an exciting discussion which might well have ended in deadlock if my class-teacher had not swung the discussion in my favour.

"It'd probably be best if Björn leaves," he said. "I don't think we should be so tied by school regulations in this special case. Björn knows what he wants to do, and perhaps we would influence his future negatively if we keep him back now. The boy has in fact actually chosen a *profession*!"

The Headmaster gives in
This made the Headmaster, whom I didn't like at all and considered a sports-hater, give in. After that meeting, Leif Dahlgren, the Swedish Tennis Association's chief coach, was brought in. He went to Södertälje, spoke to the Headmaster, and told him about the plans they had for my future. Earlier, my parents had talked of bringing in a higher authority, Eve Malmgren, for instance, the Chairman of the Association, and it was perhaps that threat that made the Headmaster weaken.

The next time I met the Headmaster was at the end of March, 1972, and I hardly recognized him. He told me I could leave school when I liked, that I could come in to classes now and again, and that I was welcome to come back when it suited me!

Since then I have never been back to school.

Janne's defeat
Directly after that meeting with the Headmaster, I went to the Swedish Tennis Association's training camp on the Riviera. I took part in several tournaments in France and Spain, defeated Jan-Erik Lundqvist 6-3, 6-2 in the Madrid Grand Prix, reached the third round in that tournament and received 3,300 kronor (£300) in prize-money, which was sent direct to the Swedish Tennis Association, as the International Tennis Association's old rule was still valid: no prize money for players under eighteen. Where the money went, however, was of no importance. I had defeated Janne Lundqvist, and had thus qualified for the Davis Cup team against New Zealand.

3. "Odd men out often reach their goals"

Many people thought I was the youngest ever Davis Cup player when at fifteen I was placed against New Zealand's number one player, Onny Parun, in May, 1972. But a journalist soon dismissed this illusion by finding that in the history of tennis I was the second youngest. Haroon Rahim from Pakistan was thirteen months younger than me when he first took on that heavy responsibility.

Onny Parun was a complicated opponent. A grass specialist who had reached the quarter-finals at Wimbledon the previous year, he was the experts' favourite and thus gave me the advantage of having nothing to lose and everything to gain. I have never been troubled by nerves and survived even this severe test. I went out on to the centre court at Båstad as if playing in any old match.

Keep the ball in play
My tactics were the simplest possible. I said to myself that I would ensure that my first service went in and I would keep the ball in play. The rest I would find out during the game. Within an hour, Parun had won the first two sets 6-4, 6-3, and I really thought that all was lost, when the match began to turn in the third set.

I knew that Parun was sensitive to pressure on his forehand and that he hated long rallies. So all the time I banked on keeping the ball in play and hoped that sooner or later he would lose his concentration.

Two hours later, I had turned a threatened defeat into a 3-2 victory by winning the last three sets 6-3, 6-4, 6-4. No great match perhaps, no glittering play or applause-winning rallies. But the Davis Cup is the Davis Cup and at the press conference afterwards I was able to talk about the greatest win of my life. There were a lot of questions, especially from one journalist who asked:

"How did you react to a faulty decision at a critical stage in the deciding set?"

I replied with the truth: that I have never been troubled by nerves and that I really am just as calm as I look. I don't know where I acquired this characteristic. Perhaps I inherited it from my parents, or perhaps when I began to study Rod Laver a few years before, a man who has wonderful concentration and never gets excited.

Without in any way trying to instruct others, I think that I have found the simplest way to success in this sport. Don't bother about the ball that's in play, but see to it that you win the next point. That doesn't mean that I always do as I say. Later on you will find that I, too, have lost control.

After my début in the Davis Cup, Jan-Erik Lundqvist wrote about me in *The Express:* "Odd men out often reach their goals." It sounded so interesting that although I usually ignore comments and newspaper articles, I was tempted to read this one.

Tennis history
Jan-Erik established first that as a fifteen

What supporters! Here showing the fine poster my school friends had done for me after my victories in my Davis Cup début

year-old I had gone down in tennis history by winning my first two Davis Cup matches. After defeating Parun, I defeated Jeff Simpson 9-7, 6-4, 5-7, 6-1. Then he praised my ability to turn 0-2 into 3-2 against Parun, and he also wrote that I would probably be playing among the international élite within four or five years. I remember that I did not always like being judged as a fifteen year-old. Talk about my age is the worst thing I know, even if I have to admit to referring to it after a defeat by an international star.

Jan-Erik also wrote:

"Björn is not an especially good tennis player. Technically an all-rounder perhaps, but nothing special. Without his physical strength, Björn would actually be just one of a crowd of juniors."

Soon after my wins over Parun and Simpson in the Davis Cup, I was defeated by Leif Johansson in an all-Sweden match (compare my defeat against Leif in the Champion Cup two years later!) and Jan-Erik Lundqvist went on about this rebuff in his article:

A sour loser

"Björn was as sour as a grey October morning after his defeat and I am not sure if he acknowledged my greeting and congratulations on his Davis Cup successes; a reaction which actually pleased me. I was like that myself after losing, and so was Lennart Bergelin, and so was Sven Davidson. It is not a question of being a bad loser, but I don't believe the sportsman exists who can laugh and be happy after a defeat."

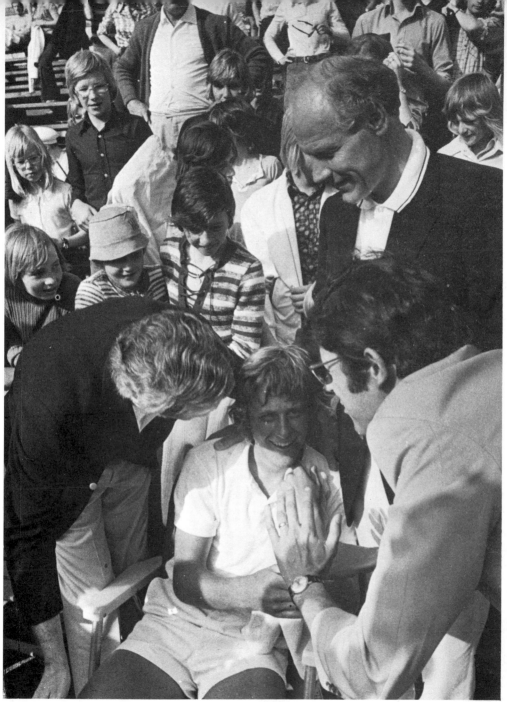

Mats Hasselquist, Lennart Bergelin and Thomas Hallberg congratulate me
after my victory over Onny Parun

4. Stubbornness is my strength

Of course, it was hard to bear losing against Leif Johansson, my neighbour and fellow-junior from Södertälje. But there was yet another defeat against Leif to come in the middle of a run of wins against him, which was even harder to bear, even harder to accept. I mean the 1-2 defeat in the Champion Cup, when I publicly protested against a faulty decision by the umpire and thus clearly surprised both the Båstad and the television audience by my behaviour.

I understand the crowd and at the same time hope they understand me. That line-call at a crucial stage in the deciding set meant a great deal, as the match was so even, and I was so anxious to win it.

Encircling the spot
I very rarely show my feelings, but this time I went over to the other side of the net and protested against the decision. I encircled with my racket the spot where the ball had touched down, but without getting any satisfaction. That particular point I could perhaps have afforded to lose. But the result of such a decision is usually that you cannot get your physical balance back for a few games, and then it is most often too late. One may well ask which of the veteran tennis champions are right—those who consider a fiery temperament a fundamental pre-requisite to reach the top, or

those who preach calm and good behaviour in all situations.

Personally I draw a sharp line between stubborn play and hot-temperedness. A player who cannot control his temper on the court will never become a great player. Occasional outbursts of anger can perhaps happen to anyone, but otherwise I am convinced that everyone gains from limiting such outbursts.

I have already touched on my strongest point, which is my persistence. I never give up in a match. However down I am, I fight on to the last ball. My list of matches shows that I have turned a great many so-called irretrievable defeats into victories. In this respect, tennis is a fantastic game. You can be hopelessly down, as long as you win the last point. I was two sets down with 0-2 against Onny Parun in the Davis Cup against New Zealand, and I won 3-2. Another example was against England's Chris Mottram in the Wimbledon Junior Final in 1972. Mottram was leading 5-2 in the deciding set, and I managed to win five games and take the set and match by 7-5.

Unnecessary defeats
Naturally there are also matches which I more or less gave away. Under the heading of "unnecessary defeats", I would put, amongst others, my 1-2 defeat against

Protesting against a decision in the Champion Cup by encircling with my
racket the spot where the ball touched down. Leif Johansson, his back
to the camera, won the match 2-1

Andrew Pattison from Rhodesia in the
Stockholm Open in 1972. The day before,
I had won against the Spaniard Andres
Gimeno by 6-3, 6-2, and was on my way
towards a clear win, when I lost nine games
in a row and lost the third and deciding set
6-4.

The same year, 1972, I also won the large
junior class in the Orange Bowl, the
biggest junior tournament in the world

after Wimbledon; won against the American Charles Pasarell in a World Championship Tennis tournament in two straight sets;
won the Swedish Championship final
against Ove Bengtson 6-4, 6-1, 6-1; and
took a set from the Australian Roy Emerson
in the American Championships.

I was sixteen, but I no longer thought of
myself as a junior. I felt I had a good chance
of winning, whoever was on the other side

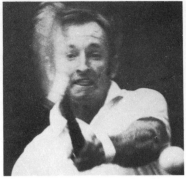

Rod Laver (*left*); Ilie Nastase (*right*)

of the net, a feeling automatic in young players who have had the opportunity of travelling round the world for a couple of years, and getting to know the person behind awe-inspiring names like Roy Emerson.

My favourites

On the other hand it is undeniable that you have favourites, players who impress you more than others. For myself, I have tried to make tennis as simple and uncomplicated as possible – "hit the ball over the net once more than your opponent" – but I am forced to admit that Rod Laver and Ilie Nastase have taught me an enormous amount.

Laver, who completely masters the art of detaching himself from the audience and the umpire and who never reveals his innermost feelings; the world's best poker-player, if he ever wished to earn a little money in that field.

Nastase the unpredictable, who hits back with a chop shot when you're expecting a top-spin lob, and who ignores all the written laws of tennis. Perhaps my most useful defeat was when he outclassed me 6-4, 6-1, 6-1, in the Monte Carlo final in April, 1973.

Full-time tennis player. Am I happy?

Yes. Imagine what it is like to earn your living at your favourite hobby, the greatest fun there is. However, all jobs have their light and dark sides, and to be honest, there have been brief periods in my tennis life when I've felt like giving up training and never again touching a racket.

The eternal grind

Training can sometimes become dreadfully dull, an eternal grind which all players have to go through and which is really one long test of your psyche. How many times have I just stopped myself from throwing down my racket in rage, when nothing goes right, when the balls go into the net or miles out! On those occasions, it is only the psychologist within me that gets me through the crisis. "Björn, you must fight your way through this training session, too. You know that it will pay off in a few months' time."

However, the best psychologist of all stands on the other side of the net – my club coach, Percy Rosberg. I have trained with him regularly ever since I moved to SALK as a fourteen year-old. Percy, who was one of Sweden's top four or five players in the 1950s, has all the qualities I appreciate in a club coach: knowledge, time and patience.

A match-free day is usually divided into two training sessions on the courts. Between this ball training, I often put in some running training, strength training and gymnastics. There is one question about my ball training that I have to reply to almost daily. When am I going to transfer to a one-handed grip on my backhand? The answer is, and always will be, never.

Christmas 1972, I won the Orange Bowl, an unofficial World Championship for Juniors. Here I am receiving the bowl

5. I have never been afraid of losing

1973 was my first great year as a tennis player, by which I do not mean I in any way became a great player. I mean that for the first time in the course of only one season, I took part in the Davis Cup, the French Championships, Wimbledon, the American Championships and I also signed a contract with World Championship Tennis.

The Davis Cup tournament, just as when we lost against Czechoslovakia in 1972, came to an abrupt end both for me and for Sweden, as Spain won without difficulty by 3-2 in Båstad. From this Davis Cup tournament I especially remember my match against Spain's number one, the shale court specialist, Manuel Orantes. I lost in three straight sets, had nothing to say about it and I recall that the whole performance was over in less than an hour.

After that setback, I had hoped for revenge against ex-professional Andres Gimeno in the second singles, but by then the result was already decided – 3-1 to Spain before the last match. Unfortunately Gimeno produced a doctor's certificate to say he was injured, just as I had gone out to warm up, and would be unable to play. Instead of Gimeno, I was placed against the Spanish Davis Cup reserve, Antonio Munoz. I won in five sets after a poor match and I

wasn't especially cheerful when I left Båstad and Sweden for another adventure – the French Championships, the world championship of shale courts. But everything changed for the better as soon as I arrived in Paris.

Failure in the Davis Cup was forgotten, and I only needed to enter the classic old Roland Garros stadium for my will to play to return. It did not matter that I drew for my first match the worst possible opponent, the American Cliff Richey, ranked seventh in the world statistics in 1972.

He goes for everything
I knew exactly which category of player I would put Cliff Richey in. I had seen him in a couple of matches when he won the giant Grand Prix tournament two years earlier; a fighter who went for every ball and sent back most of them.

Was I nervous?

The question came just as predictably in Paris as it had in all the other places at press conferences after matches. And perhaps it was a justifiable question. Shouldn't a sixteen year-old feel nervous at such a moment?

"No," I said. "I have never been troubled by nerves."

I noticed that the answer surprised them, but it was absolutely true, for sometimes a

18

Manuel Orantes was one of my toughest opponents in 1973. He defeated
me in the Davis Cup and in Toronto, before I managed to break
the sequence of losses in Nottingham

tennis player experiences from the very first ball in a match a feeling of genuine contentment.

Match of contentment

This three-set match against Cliff Richey was a typical match of contentment, one of the three or four best matches I have ever played. Everything went right, base-line strokes, service, volleys, slice shots, and I soon noticed that the eleven thousand spectators were on my side. I halted Cliff Richey with 6-3, 6-2, and after losing against Orantes in the Davis Cup a few days earlier, these were wonderful scores to send back to Sweden, where some critics had begun to question my ability and my chances of development.

But on to the next match: Pierre Barthes, Frenchman and skilled ex-professional, by whom I would "normally" have been defeated. Fortunately, however, I had managed to conserve my good form for a few more days and won against Barthes by 6-3, 1-6, 8-6, went on to the last sixteen with 6-7, 7-5, 6-2, 7-6 against Dick Stockton, and suddenly found myself face to face with the Italian number one, Adriano Panatta.

The radio appears

Clearly many people were now nosing out another sensation, because Swedish Radio among others appeared with a correspondent in Paris. And also Sweden's largest papers began to cover the French Championships with their own correspondents.

Unfortunately the match did not develop into what I had inwardly hoped for. When it eventually started, two days late because of rain, I noticed already in the first set that Panatta was a player of quite a different class from Barthes and Stockton, for instance. The Italian played wisely, carefully, held the ball in play and also appeared to be extremely professional in the decisive stage of the match. The score gives the match in a nutshell: 6-7, 6-2, 5-7, 6-7. So I lost two sets after tie-break. Seldom does a player succeed in turning a threatened defeat into victory after two tie-break losses, and in this case I wasn't even given a chance to try, as tie-break number two was the same as match-ball for Panatta.

"But if I win and he doesn't with 7-6 in the fourth set . . . No," I said to myself. "Forget such thoughts. Look ahead instead, to the next tournament."

Many people have criticised me and warned me about this insatiable appetite for the next tournament. The next and the next and the next.

But as long as the will to play is on me and I have an appetite for competitive tennis, I shall take part in as many tournaments as possible. All right, it is true that so many tournaments and matches bring about a few so-called unnecessary defeats, but I have never been afraid of losing and I'm still convinced that this constant flitting to different parts of the world, different countries, environments and people is an important part of the education of a complete tennis player.

I felt terribly small
Contact and relations with great players, for instance, are an essential part of such an education, and here I think of my début among the great stars of 1972 and the feelings I had when I arrived at Forest Hills outside New York to play against Roy Emerson in the American Championships – how terribly small I felt in the changing-rooms, faced with the sight of the international stars I had heard so much about and had admired for so long. My stomach

curled up as I went out on to the court to face Roy Emerson.

After the match, lost by 5-7, 6-4, 4-6, 4-6, I had a conversation with Emerson as if he were just anyone, and then I realised that even this international élite consisted of "ordinary" people. In this respect, and in contrast to many experts, I would like to encourage all young players in their ambition to travel and compete. The sooner you get to know the best players, both as players and people, the greater your chance of defeating them! What did I think of Roy Emerson, during that match?

Nothing free
In one respect he came up to all my expectations. He gave absolutely nothing away, not a single ball, while I gave away ten or fifteen, not from nervousness, but from respect. I was thinking about what a fantastically skilful player was standing on the other side of the net and unconsciously I overplayed many balls.

If a newcomer arrives at a large international tournament quite without preconceived ideas, I think he would find the new environment one hundred per cent problem-free. Anyhow my experiences of Emerson, Rod Laver, Ilie Nastase, Manuel Orantes and all the other international stars are wholly positive. You become one of the gang in next to no time. The established players take it in turns to give advice, keep the newcomer company at lunch or dinner, all the time feeding you with sensible and well-placed comments which strengthen your self-confidence.

Faced with the match against Cliff Richey in the French Championships, I was, for instance, enormously helped by Arthur Ashe. He kept saying that "the most important thing is to fight, to give everything" and that I shouldn't worry about who was standing on the other side of the net.

"You've everything to gain as long as you fight," Ashe said. "And actually, I give you a small chance of winning, too."

Such comments were encouraging and I had no idea that my "thanks" to him a few months later would be to knock him out of the American Championships. In the "match of my life", I defeated Ashe 6-7, 6-4, 6-4, 6-4 and reached the last sixteen to play against the player who had turned the 1973 Wimbledon upside-down, the Yugoslav, Nikola Pilic. But more about the Ashe match later on.

Ilie Nastase hits a backhand volley in the Monte Carlo final in 1973. I am standing ready on the base-line. *Right*, receiving my second prize from Princess Antoinette. Nastase won easily by 3-0

6. My life's ambition — Wimbledon

After the French Championships, a spell of total confusion reigned in the tennis world. The Yugoslavian professional player, Nikola Pilic, had been banned from the Italian Championships and Wimbledon by both the Yugoslavian and the International Tennis Association, a sentence that brought with it unimagined, not to say sensational consequences to organisers, players and spectators.

Nikola Pilic, who was and still is a member of the professionals' union, indirectly caused the most discussed tennis boycott of all time. Some other union members refused to appear at Wimbledon if the ban against Pilic were not lifted. But the sentence remained and the union implemented its threat, though with a few exceptions. After complicated negotiations and discussions, both Roger Taylor and Ilie Nastase decided to play.

Together with Ove Bengtson, I was able to watch at close quarters the exciting finale between the Wimbledon organisers and the union's spokesmen, Jack Kramer and Stan Smith, because the Swedish Wimbledon team was at that time training and playing on grass outside London.

Solidarity or play

Only one of the Swedish players was a union member; Ove Bengtson. What should he do? Show solidarity to his own union and to his union colleague, Pilic, or follow the Swedish Tennis Association's recommendation and take part in Wimbledon? Ove did not have to think very long before deciding to leave Wimbledon.

For me, however, the situation was different. I had no responsibilities to anyone apart from the Swedish Tennis Association, and I had long dreamt of a début at Wimbledon. It became a début and a tournament that I shall never forget. In the absence of professionals, I was seeded number six in the whole tournament, and I cannot explain this promotion and confidence in any other way than that the Wimbledon organisers placed most weight on what had happened at the French Championships two months earlier. Suddenly I was one of the favourites in the most famous tournament in the world.

Then came the draw: Björn Borg, Sweden, versus Premjitt Lall, India, in the first round. And then the allocation of courts: Borg versus Lall on the packed

Nikola Pilic from Yugoslavia, who indirectly caused the boycott by the professionals at Wimbledon

(15,000 spectators) centre court; a framework to my taste. I like playing before large crowds and hearing the murmur from the stands. I was both proud and grateful when, with Lall, I stepped out on to the grass and received the applause from the spectators. Hundreds of tennis players appear at Wimbledon year after year without ever getting anywhere near his or her greatest wish, to be allowed to play on the centre court. Now I was standing there on the classic "centre", as a seventeen-year-old, in my first singles match.

Ready? Play!
We were allowed a few minutes' knock-up, a few minutes to get to know each other and the Wimbledon grass, and then the slow thumping was interrupted by two words which quietly but swiftly took us

into the serious game. The umpire said "Ready? Play!" Within an hour and a half, the serious game was over.

To thunderous applause and whistles, I left the court having defeated Lall with occasional good playing by 6-3, 6-4, 9-8 (tie-break). Reasonable playing, but no great match. But the crowd was very pleased, which I had noticed during the match too, and most of all I received applause for my first service and my top-spin forehand. My first service went in every time and never before had I served so many aces, eighteen in all.

The goal is reached

My first obstacle had been cleared, the goal reached. I had no greater ambition than to survive the first round, despite being seeded number six, and from then on I experienced the wonderful feeling of being able to fight my way from an inferior position. If it had not been for the fans, the English school-girls, the continuation would have been a dare-to-win tournament quite free from pressure.

The commotion had been great even when I had first gone to London. A seeded seventeen year-old was something new in the long history of Wimbledon and I had hardly had time to unpack my cases in my hotel room before I was "attacked" by autograph hunters, journalists and photographers.

My first match, against Lall, produced further misgivings for the future. Hundreds of girls had taken the seats nearest the court and although from the very beginning I had

My first match at Wimbledon. The Indian Lall serves and I return with a forehand. I won the match by 3-0

regarded fans as genuine and spontaneous supporters, their constant applause and screams became irritating. Genuine supporters should stick to their favourites in every situation, but that didn't stop me feeling sorry when Lall did not receive applause he deserved.

"Attacked" by girls

After my 3-0 victory, when I had taken a shower, changed and was on my way to the restaurant at Wimbledon, I was "attacked" by about three hundred girls. They dragged me down on to the road and there I lay for at least a quarter of an hour without a chance of getting up. Some policemen came to my rescue, pushing their way through, helping me to my feet and escorting me to the restaurant. In the security of a police escort, I realised that it was going to be hard work with these girls.

Was I scared? Well, yes, I was a little, as I lay there in the dust on the street with girls all over me. But it was fun, too, to be appreciated. It was all new to me, as I had never experienced anything like it before. On the day after my match against Lall and battle with London's schoolgirls, came another and even more difficult one – the match against London's fickle sportswriters.

"A star is Bjorn"

I usually never waste my time reading about myself, but here was my picture and my name in such enormous letters on the sports pages that I couldn't avoid the headlines. In most papers I had even stolen space on the front pages. One leading sports writer, Peter Wilson, wrote under giant headlines A STAR IS BJORN, a pun on Judy Garland's film *A Star is Born*, in Europe's largest daily paper, the *Daily Mirror*, and in the *Daily Telegraph*, another sporting expert called Lance Tingay wrote:

"Seldom has one had such great expectations of such a young player and seldom have those expectations been so fulfilled. . . . This impudent young man stepped into the centre court as if he had lived there all his life and gave the crowd a brilliant display of tennis. He began as a Wimbledon novice and ended as the favourite. His maturity is astonishing. It was also the strength in his service and his fluent sweeping forehand which gave him so many swingeing winning balls."

Down to earth

I can't imagine where English sports writers find all their grand words and fantastic sentences. But I did understand that "it was a question of not believing you were half so good, and of going on training like the beginner you are!" Anyhow, on my side I had a reliable coach and trainer who always brought me down to earth after a win; that great player, Lennart Bergelin.

"Remember that you had bloody good luck and least of all played well," was his standard comment during those hectic Wimbledon days.

Rosewall defeated

But on to round three and my meeting with the West German, Karl Meiler, who earlier in the season had defeated both Roger Taylor, seeded number two at Wimbledon after Nastase, and Ken Rosewall. The match was as even and uncertain as I had feared and although I won both the first

The girls were hard work at Wimbledon. *Above*, surrounded after my win over Lall; *below*, surrounded on the court after a doubles match

Against the West German Karl Meiler in the third round, I was in a bad way. *Above*, he hits a forehand; *below*, I reply with the same stroke

and second sets 6-4, I was in a bad way. Meiler came back, without effort won the third and fourth sets 6-3, 6-2, and led by 1-0 in the fifth and deciding set when I at last came out of my down spell. I began to limit my net attacks, to keep the ball in play in a different way and after being 0-1 down, took three of Meiler's service games.

With 6-3 in the deciding set, I had won my first big match on one of Wimbledon's side courts and when I compared my two introductory victories, I valued the second one considerably more.

"Borg's Brigade"

The reason for this was not that Meiler is a better player than Lall, but because the schoolgirls, the fans whom the English press called Borg's Brigade, came so close to me in the second match that they influenced my playing. Of course, the girls did it to support me as I went through the crisis in the third and fourth set, but at the same time it was unbelievably distracting constantly hearing their comments; calls that often had nothing to do with the play itself, but referred only to my appearance and what the girls felt for me. On the side courts, the spectators almost stand on the court, and although I did my best to detach myself from my surroundings, it remained an intention only. I *was* irritated just as much as my opponent was, and when the horde of girls continued outside the courts, I began to find the tumult a torment. I couldn't even walk the usual routes at Wimbledon, but constantly had to use up energy trying to find different ways to get to places.

Fortunately, Lennart Bergelin had managed to book a room in a hotel for me and I didn't have to live in the big players' hotel, but managed to get rid of most of the fans in the evenings by taking the tube or a taxi to a pleasant place some miles outside the city.

The hotel – happiness

Happiness can mean a great deal in life, and during Wimbledon it was my little hotel room. Every evening, I looked forward to it, an intense feeling brought about by the fact that I was the girls' legitimate prey even on the streets of London. As soon as I showed myself, they appeared, twenty or thirty of them, and began "pawing" me.

My thoughts were now circling round these girls as much as round the tournament. I appealed to the organisers to excuse me the side courts in future, and to dampen the girls' enthusiasm, I had myself photographed with my club and mixed-doubles partner, Helena Anliot. The organisers replied with a promise that the guard would be strengthened, and the day after that, the picture of Helena and me appeared in the *Daily Mirror*, the caption exactly what I had hoped it would be: *Björn Borg and his girlfriend.*

Unfortunately neither the picture nor Helena provided the protection I had hoped for. English schoolgirls did not care a bit whether I had a girlfriend or not and I had to go on reckoning with the walk from the changing room to the restaurant taking at least half an hour.

Denying the romance

Gradually the picture of Helena and me found its way into the Swedish papers, with the caption translated into Swedish, which had not been my intention at all. So

The picture that was to dampen the enthusiasm of the fans – with Helena Anliot

now I had to spend even more time *denying* the romance.

All clear for the next match – against the Hungarian Szabolcs Baranyi in the fourth round. I was allocated a side court again, and again the fans had taken the "strategic" seats, so once again I was faced with two opponents, Baranyi and my own psyche. Just as in the Mailer match, I started well, almost too well, I thought, with such a highly skilled and steady player as Baranyi on the other side of the net.

Match balls
With little difficulty, I won the first two sets 6-3, 6-2, and then was as close to a 3-0 win as I could get. Three match points! Two of them the Hungarian countered with a couple of very skilful manoeuvres and the third I gave away. A straight backhand at Baranyi instead of a backhand-cross and fifteen minutes later, I had lost the set 6-8. Just as against Meiler, I found myself in a crisis in the middle of the match and had

nothing to offer when it came to the tough fourth set. Baranyi evened up with 7-5, and, faced with the last and deciding set, I knew that the result of the first game would probably be vital, either the trip home or the quarter-finals against Roger Taylor.

I won that first and psychologically important game, and after 2-0 and 3-0, Baranyi more or less gave up; the final score was 6-1. Afterwards, everyone wanted to know why in game after game, set after set, I stubbornly went on hitting at Baranyi's backhand, his very best weapon.

My legs gave out
I answered honestly that I never thought about where I placed my balls and established later that my legs had begun to give out in the fourth set and I was perhaps suffering from a virus which caused me to feel so tired. My condition under normal circumstances is very good and I could find only two explanations for my lost form and backsliding for two sets running; one, a

29

virus and two, psychic fatigue.

I never found out what happened. Perhaps I should have seen a doctor and had a thorough examination. But how could I have fitted that into my already overcrowded existence? Now I accepted only those invitations which interested me and were to my advantage as a full-time tennis player, an attitude which entailed leaving a bundle of telegrams in my hotel room unopened, and I only opened and glanced through a second bunch.

Another Osmond

Some of the telegrams contained offers of recordings, and I know that Europe's largest record company had advanced plans to make me into another Donny Osmond – what a thought, when you consider that my favourites in that field are Elvis Presley and Shirley Bassey!

And then Radio Luxemburg wanted me to say a few words to the girl listeners on an evening pop programme. And then all those business men who invited me to come to their stores and shops to autograph photographs . . . I had telegrams of this kind every day, but did not reply to a single one.

Living advertisement

The combination of tennis player and living advertisement is, however, worth while for a few years, if I can rise a couple of classes as a player and thus create a more advantageous negotiating position. As I win and advance in tournaments, the offers pour in and it would of course be stupid to tie oneself to a particular concern or a particular sum, if one can make very much more money by waiting!

Well, perhaps my development will now stop and I have reached the culmination of my career as a tennis player, so there will be no more offers. But I can take that risk, just as I took an even greater risk when I left school.

During Wimbledon, my programme was full from morning to night. Here being interviewed by Swedish Television's Bengt Grive

7. A defeat I remember

I seldom remind myself of defeats, but there are few matches I remember as well as my defeat by the Englishman, Roger Taylor, in the quarter-finals at Wimbledon. It was a match of great swings each way, of a strange decision by the umpire, a match that ended and then continued again, a match in which the loser was applauded as victor as much as the winner, a quarter-final that involved England and Sweden equally, as it was televised in both countries and the papers next day devoted whole pages to the television drama.

And it was certainly a dramatic match, after I had finally joined in the action. The introduction was not exactly what I had expected. I usually like playing against left-handers, but during the first quarter of an hour, Taylor stood like a wall at the net, killing dead ninety per cent of my returns and winning the set 6-1.

Ice in my stomach
Changing ends and continuing after being outclassed in that way was uncomfortable, but the most important thing in such circumstances is to keep a cool head, play with ice in your stomach, and not show by the slightest flicker of an eyelid that your opponent is making an impression on you.

In the second set, my first service began to work a little better, my net attacks paid dividends, and Taylor's base strokes went out now and again. The second set was mine, 8-6, and when I won the third too, I knew that being outclassed in the first set was only a temporary setback.

It was possible to shake Taylor after all, and if only I could keep the game and my legs going, I stood a good chance of winning the match. I even began to believe I might win when my play continued to go well at the start of the fourth set. But then I lost my grip as quickly as it had returned before, from one point to the next, and Taylor could haul himself up and proceed to an easy win, 6-3.

Then for the third time running, I faced a fifth and deciding set, a set which from the point of view of excitement and drama was beyond anything else I had encountered. Perhaps the whole match was decided at fifteen-all in the first game, the game I have always regarded as the key to victory.

The chalk flies
Fifteen-all and I hit a ball that fell on the middle of the sideline so that the chalk flew. Unfortunately this wasn't seen by the umpire, who called thirty-fifteen to Taylor, instead of fifteen-thirty. It was one of the very few faulty decisions in this match and

From my defeat by Roger Taylor at Wimbledon. *Left*, the Englishman
has dropped his racket during one of our duels. *Right*, I leave the centre
court with a broken racket

Taylor, I, and the spectators were surprised that one could be made on a ball that was so easy to see. In a similar situation in the third set, I had corrected a faulty decision to Taylor's advantage and now naturally I hoped that Taylor would reciprocate the courtesy and correct the umpire. Imagine my surprise when I saw Taylor throw out his arms with a resigned gesture and the decision remained.

Afterwards I learned that Taylor had told both the linesmen and the umpire that the ball had touched down in the middle of the line, that the umpire had refused to change his decision, and that Taylor had not insisted that the ball should be played again or judged to be in my favour.

Down by 1-5

I don't know what happened after this incident. A moment later, I realised that Taylor had won that psychologically vital first game and had then gone ahead to take the lead by 5-1. The way the set continued was almost too sensational to be true. After an upward surge beginning with saving two match-points at 1-5, I caught up to 5-5, was forty-thirty on my own service, when for the third time in this match, I was called for foot-fault. Foot-fault, which had never happened to me before.

Taylor then took both mine and his own service games and won the set and match by 7-5. The end of the match is almost a chapter in itself. Taylor was 6-5, forty-thirty and was given game, set and match by the umpire on a faulty service. The ball hit the ground quite a way outside the service square, and at this point Roger Taylor showed what a fantastically good sportsman he is. Instead of thanking me for the match, picking up his things and leaving the court, he corrected the umpire, ordered me to go on playing, taking the risk of 7-5 being transformed to 6-6, and with that the risk of losing the whole match.

What I did wrong and when I lost my grip in this match, I will never really know. They are questions which will grind on, even if the true explanation is that I was beaten by a better player.

The charm of tennis
But that is tennis, and therein lies also the charm of the sport. And anyhow, how many grounds would Taylor have had for self-reproach if he had lost the fifth set and the match, when he was leading 5-1, ordering me to play on when victory was his, before that having missed several match points!

It is true I never give up in a match, a fact I was careful to point out at the press conference afterwards, but when I was on an up again, I did in fact have luck with two or three important points. It is easy to forget the facts and of course I could easily have lost in the fifth set.

Roger Taylor was hero-worshipped by a united press for his sportsmanship the following day and to a question on what the hero thought of his defeated opponent, his answer was:

"Björn Borg is well-trained, quick and aggressive in his play, and in addition behaves very well on the court."

It was nicely said by a winner who directly after the match was forced to look on as "Borg's Brigade" stormed on to the court and paid homage to the loser as if he were the victor. To sum up, I can say that it was difficult to swallow my defeat, but easy to congratulate Roger Taylor.

Correcting the umpire?
Long after the Wimbledon tournament, I thought about that strange decision in the match between Taylor and me. Is it right for a player to correct the umpire? Is it certain that your opponent will be as generous when he has the opportunity to reciprocate the courtesy? Isn't it much simpler to obey the umpire's directive and rely on the fact that good luck and bad luck, including faulty decisions, equal out in the end?

In the future, I have decided to "judge" from case to case. If an obvious faulty decision is made in the middle of a match, then I will request that the point is played again. If, as in Taylor's case, I then won the match on a faulty decision at forty-thirty, then of course the point cannot be replayed. That would mean another match point. No, then I would recommend continuing from deuce instead.

8. A steady girlfriend not for me

It was with mixed feelings that I left London and Wimbledon to get into trim for shale courts again for my next big tournament, Båstad's Grand Prix. I had indeed looked forward to the day when I would be flying to Copenhagen and Båstad, leaving behind the hectic life and stress of London. But when the day arrived, after my defeat by Taylor, I also felt a sense of loss and inner emptiness which I had never expected.

There was something special about Wimbledon and London, not least the girls and fans who, although they had been troublesome, had given me unforgettably positive and festive memories. I would apply for Wimbledon the following year, but as I was packing my cases at the hotel, I knew that no Wimbledon of the future would ever be like the professional-free summer of 1973.

It was easy to touch on the subject of tennis and girls in those memorable days in London, and I was not thinking only of the schoolgirls who constantly kept me company, however unwilling I was. Every day I saw several of my friends, colleagues and opponents together with women, often so-called "steady girlfriends", and each time I saw this, I thought to myself "don't let it happen to me!"

A bad combination

Tennis and a steady girlfriend do not make a good combination, as the history of tennis can produce plenty of evidence to show, and I myself am convinced that my career as a tennis player will come to an end the moment I feel as much for a girl as I do for that little white ball. Perhaps it sounds somewhat foolish, but for a young man on his way up in tennis, who has also decided to earn his living that way, there is no choice. Wait! Wait, if you don't want everything you have built up to collapse.

A single-minded and ambitious man has no time for a steady girlfriend, not to mention marriage, if he is to succeed as a tennis player. I have seen the consequences when a team of men are away or abroad, playing in tournaments for two or three months. The friend who gets love-letters suffers from homesickness after a couple of weeks and cannot concentrate on training or on the matches.

The most difficult and hardest part of the job of being a tennis player is not the matches, nor the training. It is the planning, the looking-ahead when you are packing your cases, booking tickets, hotel rooms and a great many other things which directly influence the results on the court.

35

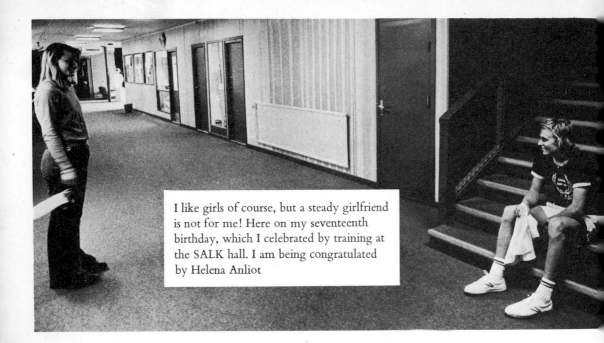

I like girls of course, but a steady girlfriend is not for me! Here on my seventeenth birthday, which I celebrated by training at the SALK hall. I am being congratulated by Helena Anliot

Training

If I make a mistake looking up in the flight timetable, I miss a connection and am late. That affects my training and my sleep, and may well make all the difference between defeat and victory. No two tennis stadiums are alike, all surfaces demand careful preparation, and you should preferably spend time studying your opponents.

I am not particularly pedantic, but three things I always hold strictly to:

1. Nine hours' sleep before important matches.
2. At least two hours' ball training every day, even when my match is on the programme.
3. Proper food, preferably a good steak every day, and always a meal an hour or so before a match.

Perhaps all players are not so particular about times and sleep as I am, but the fact is I live according to my own recipe for the sake of survival. I simply can't play if I haven't had enough sleep the night before. This also explains why I sometimes surprise people by leaving, for instance, a party or a late dinner in the middle of the dessert. The following day it has happened that I have been standing on the court in a temperature of 35 degrees Centigrade, thanking my better instinct for insisting on leaving early the night before. I am also convinced that it isn't just opportunities and fighting spirit that have given me so many wins in deciding sets.

The good life

Otherwise it is easy to fall for the good life

A steak and music from my tape-recorder are part of fuelling for a match

if you are a more or less established player. Everywhere, organisers and supporters tempt you with evening parties which often go on into the small hours, and if you once cease sticking to your principles and give in "for just an hour", then the next morning's training invariably suffers for it.

Perhaps it is my rock-hard principles that have produced the picture of Björn Borg as a lone wolf. Not everyone has the impression that I am a loner going my own way, but to be honest I have nothing against being on my own with my own thoughts. First and foremost, I am dependent on having a calm spell on my own after a defeat. Otherwise I consider myself a typical teenager, one of the most ordinary.

9. Regular salary and free flights

After successes in the French Championships and Wimbledon, I was very conscious of the fact that again I had to make an important decision. After leaving school, I had developed more rapidly than I had dared hope for and the fact that this was appreciated by my employers, the Swedish Tennis Association, was only too clear. Invitations poured in and the problem was no longer one of finding tournaments but of choosing the right ones in collaboration with the Association. But should I as a sixteen year-old (in the spring and early summer of 1973) tie myself down so much abroad that in future there would be no time for the Stockholm Open, Båstad's Grand Prix, the Davis Cup etc?

The big money
The really big money lies outside Sweden, and although it has always been my ambition to hasten slowly, there came a point when I realised that I could no longer afford to miss the opportunity called World Championship Tennis. In 1972, I had been invited to join Ove Bengtson in the WCT gang, but after discussions with the Tennis Association, I decided to decline the offer.

A year later, I could no longer afford to refuse. I felt mature enough to join the professionals and was convinced that even a series of defeats would benefit my develop-ment. Perhaps it was when faced with the fact that Swedish tennis would lose its hold on me, that the Tennis Association brought out their big and surprising project so swiftly. I say project, as I had no idea what was going on, although I had had a tip that *something* would happen after Wimbledon.

As far back as during the French Championships, Mats Hasselquist had urged me to deal with someone else apart from the Tennis Association about the future. Shortly before my trip to London and Wimbledon, Hasselquist reiterated his theme, this time with considerably greater force.

Contract
If I would just keep all my interests in check for a while and not sign any binding agreement, then the Tennis Association would "try to arrange some form of contract" when I returned from Wimbledon. My curiosity was great, but I never thought in terms of an agreement which would be so advantageous all round.

From 1st August, 1973, I was to be employed as an official of the airline, SAS, Scandinavian Air Services, with a regular monthly salary for five years, and with free flights all over the world. In return, I was to play in all the big Swedish tournaments, the Stockholm Open, Davis Cup, Champion Cup, Båstad's Grand Prix, a Swedish

The SAS contract is signed. I thank Mats Hasselquist of the Swedish
Tennis Association and Yngve Wessman, Director of SAS

championship per year, plus the King's Cup.

Naturally I gave a great deal of thought to the project and I had long discussions with my parents and the Tennis Association. When the decision had to be taken, however, I could think of no reason for refusing the offer.

Secure future

In practice, I now had a financially secure future, a job which was renewable at the end of five years, and I could still join World Championship Tennis in the biggest tournaments in the world. My gratitude knew no limits when I signed the agreement, and the whole idea, which had been Mats Hasselquist's, was carried through. The man who gave the final all-clear for the SAS part in it had probably been Marcus Wallenberg, a member of the SAS Board of Directors and honorary Chairman of the Tennis Association.

The job itself entailed visiting SAS offices all over the world on my tennis trips and in that way trying to learn the job and bring the company new customers. Compared with other officials in the sales department, the difference was that I was to learn the job from the outside, while other new employees started from home.

All clear to WCT

Directly after the agreement with SAS and the Tennis Association, I gave the all-clear to World Championship Tennis about turning professional from January 1974 onwards. Before that, I had been involved in long discussions with the Tennis Association, for or against joining WCT. At first the Association had urged me to sign a contract with a new indoor circuit in the USA, Bill Riordan's circuit, which takes place between January and March. I was just as convinced that the best opponents would be found in WCT's tournaments from January to April, and finally we agreed. "Well, you can decide for yourself where and in which tournaments you're going to play!"

39

10. The greatest success of all time

The boycott of Wimbledon by the professionals, as I mentioned before, created almost total confusion in the tennis world, and one of the organisations which felt the ground swaying beneath it at the time was the Swedish Tennis Association. What would happen in the 1973 Båstad Grand Prix? I don't know how many times Mats Hasselquist telephoned Lennart Bergelin during Wimbledon, but anyhow the starting field was so thin a week before the opening that not just Lennart, but all the Swedish players in London were more or less commissioned to recruit international stars to Båstad.

Two weeks before the opening at Wimbledon, I heard that players like Stan Smith, Ilie Nastase and Manuel Orantes were as good as fixed, but the nearer the Båstad organisers came to the draw, the thinner the lists grew.

The draw is moved
In this situation, Hasselquist and Co. had no choice. The draw was postponed for a few days and the result, as most people still remember, was the best starting field that had ever occurred at Båstad, not least from the financial point of view.

When the draw at last took place, it no longer mattered that Nastase had tied himself to a tournament in Switzerland and that the Wimbledon champion Jan Kodes from Czechoslovakia withdrew owing to an injury and returned home to Prague. Stan Smith and Manuel Orantes were fixed and also the Yugoslav, Nikola Pilic, the man behind the Wimbledon boycott! The organisers also ensured that the young Björn Borg might pull in a few spectators.

In the draw, I was placed against India's Anand Amritraj in the first match, and got close to winning this apparently somewhat uncertain match without losing a game, but slackened off a few minutes in each set, so had to be content with 6-1, 6-4. Anyhow, the opening of play was much easier than I had expected, and I was looking forward with confidence to my next match, against Jan Kukal from Czechoslovakia.

Cold shower
The came the cold shower. I had been expecting it for a very long time and yet it was still considerably more unpleasant than I had feared. My play had been up and down during most of Wimbledon and so I knew that my form could come back and vanish just as quickly in Båstad, too. But I hadn't calculated on a whole match of bad play,

The 1973 Båstad final watched by me as a spectator high up on the television stand

and that came against Kukal. He won the first set 7-6 after tie-break, and in the second set I was in such a bad position several times that a large proportion of the crowd (4,000 spectators) grew tired of my misses and moved over to the other courts.

But I was determined to win this match, and with some luck and fighting spirit succeeded in doing so with another tie-break, 7-6. In the third and deciding set, I had the pleasure of seeing my lost spectators returning and after another half an hour, the crisis was over, 6-3.

The sting returns
My favourable draw had now brought me into the quarter-finals against Chile's Jaime Pinto Bravo, and just as swiftly as I had lost the sting in my service and forehand, I got it back again. The score was 6-3, 6-1, and as another Swede, Leif Johansson, had taken one of the semi-final places (each worth 10,000 kronor), (£1,000) the tournament looked like becoming one of the greatest gate-successes of all time.

The day of the semi-finals also confirmed that two international stars against two Swedes was the ideal attraction. Although play was being televised live, the interest in the two matches, Leif Johansson versus Manuel Orantes, and Björn Borg versus Stan Smith, was so great that the Tennis Stadium was sold out an hour before the first match.

The organisers say that at least 1,000 spectators were turned away at the gates and at the press conference afterwards they asserted that not even old Båstad favourites like Jan-Erik Lundqvist and Ulf Schmidt had been able to concentrate interest to that extent. Unfortunately, the semi-finals did not become what the great television public expected.

Leif stood no chance whatsoever against Orantes and lost in three straight sets, and I was equally lost when Stan Smith produced the best play he has ever shown on shale courts. The score of 4-6, 4-6, 2-6 perhaps does not look all that hopeless, but the truth is that he never gave me a shadow of a chance.

In the final against Orantes, Stan Smith continued to play world championship tennis, won three sets to nil, and once again I received a useful reminder of what a very long way it is to the top.

11. Broader context — better tennis

Three months later, however, I was able once again to hit against players in the top half of the list of the ten best players in the world. With Ove Bengtson and Rolf Norberg, I started a long Canadian and American tour with the Canadian Championships in Toronto. The tournament was played on very fast shale courts and as early as in the first match, against Pat Cramer from South Africa, I noticed that the surface suited me as well as the smooth grass of Wimbledon. The opposition also spurred me on and kindled the competitive spark.

After Båstad's Grand Prix, I had lost in the first round of a Grand Prix tournament in Kitzbuhl, Austria, won two matches and lost one (to Leif Johansson) in the Champion Cup, and taken altogether five titles in the Swedish Senior and Junior Championships. None of the latter three tournaments gave me an opportunity to meet the big stars, and this was reflected in my standard of play. Although I prepare for a match in the Swedish Junior Championships just as thoroughly as for a match at Wimbledon, my playing style is strongly influenced by the opposition.

More relaxed
In a larger context, I am more relaxed and my tennis is quite simply better. Pat Cramer, ranked number two in South Africa, gave me no particular trouble and after occasional very good play, I lost only six games, 6-4, 6-2.

Australia's Dick Crealy was my next opponent, a player who had won Båstad's international week in 1970, and also had contracted to join World Championship Tennis. Again my repertoire of strokes functioned and for the first time for a long time, I felt that my legs were carrying me through all difficulties. Balls that had been untakeable a few weeks earlier, I not only managed to reach, but also to return well-placed. "Everything worked," I wrote in my notebook, after I had given Crealy an even worse game than Cramer, 6-2, 6-3. By this win, I had reached the last sixteen in this championship, and yet that step forward was not what was occupying my thoughts.

Against my idol
In my next match, I was to be playing for the first time against one of the greatest players in the history of the game and one of my childhood's great idols – Ken Rosewall. The last sixteen in a large championship was an excellent opportunity. I was on top form then and had everything to gain against a star who, although thirty-eight years old, still ranked third in the world. The match

In the Outdoor Swedish Championships, I won everything I took part in. Singles (*right*, thanking Tenny Svensson for the match). Doubles (with Tenny Svensson), and Mixed Doubles (*below*, playing a forehand and Helena Anliot watching). *Above left*, photographed with Isabelle Larsson, who won the Ladies Singles

against Rosewall was played on the centre court before about four thousand spectators, and it was the best I had hitherto played, and the most remarkable.

Everything went well in the first set, my service, volley, my top-spin backhand, and my legs carried me to the most impossible places. All my friends and supporters agreed with me afterwards that I had never played more complete tennis. I had played at the peak of my ability for the whole set and the only thing I wasn't satisfied with was the score.

Deuce in every game

Rosewall had won 6-2, despite the fact that it had been deuce in every game. Then I went on playing well, and in the second set presumably even better as almost without exception I got back decisive balls to even the score by 6-1. I could hardly believe it when the set score 1-1 went up on the board and the enthusiastic crowd applauded wildly.

The third set was my best ever. I have never served so well, never got to so many drop shots, never had my double-handed backhand been so effective and never have I fought more successfully. Rosewall led 3-1 and then 5-3, but I always came back and the end was actually pretty fantastic. I took three games running and won the set and match 7-5. The spectators were standing on their seats screaming as the match point was played.

Afterwards, Rosewall said "Well played, boy," and that was a comment which warmed me, as it came from a player who really can distinguish between good and bad tennis. I *had* played well and I had beaten

Ken Rosewall. Can one get any better?

In the quarter-final, another shale specialist was waiting; Manuel Orantes, the Spanish number one who had outclassed me in the Davis Cup.

One class since Båstad

I still felt confident playing on the centre court, and even if I didn't play as well as against Rosewall, I don't think either the organisers or the crowd were disappointed. Orantes won in two straight sets, 7-5, 7-6 (tie-break) but said afterwards that he was playing at the peak of his ability and that I had moved up at least one class since we had met at Båstad.

From the quarter-final, I also remember saving a lot of match points at 3-5 and 4-5 in the second set, that I went up from 5-6 to 6-6, and then lost the tie-break at 7-5. I was more than content when I left Toronto and Canada for New York and the USA for the next big competition.

My childhood idol, Ken Rosewall, whom I managed to defeat in Toronto

12. "Not a chance," said Ashe

The American Championships, after Wimbledon, is considered the most famous grass court tournament in the world. For a second time, I was in this huge gathering of stars, fully aware that the order of play would be of the greatest importance. Exactly a year before, I had drawn against Roy Emerson in the first round, and although at the time I didn't play too bad a match, the whole adventure in Forest Hills was over in a couple of hours. This time I was in luck!

With no grass training, I came up against the American Roy Barth in my first match. I played unbelievably badly on the unfamiliar surface, but nevertheless managed to turn a threatened defeat into a safe win. Barth won the first two sets by 6-3, 7-6, but from then on it was sufficient for me to keep the ball in play to take three straight sets, 6-4, 6-1, 6-2. The match against Barth was played on the centre court before quite a large crowd, and when I left the court I felt genuinely sorry that the spectators had only occasionally seen any really good tennis.

The invaluable Bergelin

Lack of familiarity with the surface was a severe handicap to me and several times, both before and after the match, my thoughts went to our Association captain, Lennart Bergelin. He had often, and with

justification, preached that "the kids must learn to travel and play on their own", but in the American Championships Lennart had been invaluable in arranging training times and courts. Bergelin has fantastic contacts all over the world and is the man who has given Rolf Norberg, Ove Bengtson, myself and other Swedes the opportunity of grass training in New York.

I met the Frenchman Jean-Baptiste Chanfreau in the second round, on one of the side courts in fearful heat (35 degrees Centigrade.) We played four long and extremely demanding sets, a hard test of condition, which I survived surprisingly well. Another victory, 7-5, 2-6, 6-2, 6-4, and an observation which strengthened my self-confidence in the face of my next match. I was beginning to make friends with the ball again, my judgement of distances was functioning, I went for the ball at the right moment and at last began to get some length.

Adjustment

Despite the shortage of courts and training times, I adjusted relatively swiftly from Toronto's shale courts to Forest Hills' faster grass. But would my "training-passes" against Barth and Chanfreau be enough? The order of play and the draw revealed that the number three seed,

45

Lennart Bergelin is invaluable as a fixer of training sessions and courts

Arthur Ashe, was my opponent in the third round; Ashe, with fresh victories behind him in two professional tournaments in 1973, number two in the American professional championships and number two in WCT's latest marathon tournament. I also knew that Ashe had won the American Championships at Forest Hills in 1968, forcing Ilie Nastase to five sets in the final of the same competition in 1972. Ashe himself said just before this tournament: "This is usually my competition. I always play well here."

Volley player
I had no special tactics in mind as I went on to the centre court before stands packed with about eleven thousand spectators. It was really sufficient to say silently to oneself "Arthur Ashe", who in his most inspired moments is the best volley-player in the world. I would have to take the balls as they came, try to pass him when he was at the net, and attack if he drew back. In the heat, at least 35 degrees Centigrade, it was an amazingly exciting match, with Ashe leading in every set. I remember every point.

First set: He broke direct, took my service and 1-0 in games at first changeover. A bad start, which I soon retrieved, however. I quite simply broke back, equalling, and at the same time feeling that all was well: "Shots good, legs good and playing mood excellent" I wrote in my notes afterwards. But that didn't stop Ashe taking the

The match against Arthur Ashe. I am serving and Ashe replies with a backhand return

set 7-6 (5-3 in tie-break).

Second set: Ashe in the lead 2-1 when I broke back. Then I held my service, broke again and won the set 6-4.

Third set: One of my most amazing retrievals. Ashe led by 3-1, had his own service and should have won the set if he had got 4-1. But in some strange way, I managed to break when it was most needed, managed to hang on with 2-3 and won with seven or eight killing passes, by 6-4.

Fourth set: I knew Ashe was shaken and that a sensation was not far off. I played winning tennis which neither I nor the crowd had previously experienced, and not even Ashe's enormous stretch was sufficient to stop my top-spin forehands and back-hands. But Ashe led 2-1 and had the service. Then the game set and match slid over towards me, and I had three match points at 5-3 on his service. Ashe played very well, saved the match points and took the game. My turn to serve at 5-4, a great chance to serve home both the set and match. An ace at thirty-all. Match point. First service in, Ashe returns on the backhand, forehand volley, forehand from Ashe – into the net! I left the court extremely happily after that victory, aware that I had played well, that the spectators were content, and also Ashe had spontaneously congratulated me with: "An excellent match, I never had a chance."

Everything succeeds
At the same time, I saw how disappointed Ashe was over his defeat, seeded number three in his favourite tournament and then knocked out by a junior from Sweden.

In the next match I was to meet Nikola Pilic from Yugoslavia, a match that would demand all my concentration and attention. The day before the match against Pilic, I said to some journalists: "I stand a good chance. I like playing against left-handers."

What I hadn't reckoned with was that Pilic was still one of the best players in the world and in his most inspired moments played fantastically well, and his match against me was one of those moments.

Pilic was the best
Pilic was better; it was as simple as that, and won 6-4, 5-7, 6-3, 6-4. But in sporting behaviour, I was way ahead of him. There always seem to be incidents when Pilic is on the court and he had both long and brief altercations with the umpire and the crowd. I will not go into details, but will content myself by repeating here one of Pilic's charming comments to the spectators:

"Bloody capitalists."

Pilic's remarks, however, did not throw my rhythm or make me lose my concentration. He won exclusively because of his better tennis.

13. Forced into a secret number

My place in the last sixteen of the American Championships produced five thousand kronor (£500), a gilt-edged cheque which made up for my defeat against Nikola Pilic. That is routine in most tournaments. The prize money is available as soon as you are knocked out. The cheque can be cashed at any bank, so any worries about pocket-money have long since ceased. Naturally, I always have to pay for food and lodging, whoever is arranging the tournament or wherever in the world it is taking place, but as a full-time SAS official, I fly free of charge nowadays. My salary has meant that I have been able to devote much more attention to my clothes and my collection of cassettes.

Clothes

A few years ago I was only mildly interested in clothes, but the more I travel and the more people I meet, the greater is my need for the latest clothes – jeans, denim jackets and matching shirts. And I have also collected quite a good assortment of tapes for my tape-recorder, sixty to seventy cassettes worth about 2,500 kronor (£250).

But what would you really like, Björn? Everywhere I go, I am asked that question. What am I going to do, which means buy, when/if the big money begins to come in?

Naturally, I would like to avoid it all by giving an evasive answer like "I haven't thought about that yet". But I don't work like that. For the last two or three years I have dreamt of having a Mercedes sports car, a 450 SL. A dream-car like that costs about 90,000 kronor (£9,000). I don't know whether it is its lines or its comfort that tempts me, or perhaps it is the horse-power under its bonnet. Anyhow, I have made up my mind, and hope to be able to realise my dream next year, when I get my driving licence.

Otherwise money seems to be a much used word all over the world, not least in the USA, where I stayed with American families for a large part of the autumn of 1973. Tennis players usually live in hotels during their tours, but organisers sometimes take upon themselves the extra responsibility and cost of finding accommodation for certain players in private houses. I have often taken advantage of this.

Snacks from the fridge

There are many advantages. It's cheaper. You always have someone to talk to. You can get snacks from the fridge and the larder (!) You can get away from tennis in between matches and training. There are few disadvantages. If you are unlucky, you land up in a family with two or three kids

On to more tournaments. Here I am sitting at Arlanda Airport in Stockholm, waiting to check in

round about ten years old who cling to you and chatter every day. But living with an American family is usually very interesting, although the conversation is often about money and finances. What are the taxes in Sweden like? How do you live? What do your parents do? Wouldn't you be better off if you moved to the USA?

I always reply correctly to all their questions, saying that Sweden is Sweden, and that I've never even given the idea of emigrating a thought.

Ignorance of Sweden
During the autumn of 1973, I lived and toured with Rolf Norberg, and both of us were surprised at first by how little Americans knew about Sweden. It wasn't so bad to hear Copenhagen called the capital of Sweden, but it felt strange to have to inform people that we had a social-democratic government, that we had had one for a long time and that the Prime Minister was called Olof Palme.

We also talked about tennis a great deal, of course, which was inevitable. The Americans then looked surprised when I told them we had snow and frost in the winter and that Swedish players are forced to play indoors to keep on form. Americans didn't pry into my intimate life, but I told them what the consequences of my recent successes were to the Borg family apartment in Södertälje – four or five girls ringing up every evening, wanting to talk about tennis and/or go out with me. My mother, who has to take most of the calls, began to get a bit irritated. In fact, so irritated that we had to get an ex-directory number.

14. A decimetre from final victory

My victories over Ken Rosewall and Arthur Ashe in the Canadian and American Championships were soon cabled round the world and this had repercussions. I didn't realise this until a tournament in Alamo, outside San Francisco, in September, 1973. I was in fact aware that I was now among the thirty best players in the world, but I was shocked all the same when the seeding was announced. First Stan Smith, second Arthur Ashe, third Tom Gorman, fourth Roy Emerson, fifth Roscoe Tanner, sixth Björn Borg, seventh John Alexander and eighth Cliff Drysdale. Was I really regarded as a better player than Drysdale and Australia's new star, Alexander? Yes, I was! This meant that I needn't risk meeting any of the best players in the first or second rounds.

Luck on my side
I was drawn against the Czech Mila Holecek in the first match, an opponent who was just as difficult as I had imagined. True, I was on an upward swing in form, but without a bit of luck that tournament would have been an unhappy story. Holecek won the first set 6-3, and then I managed to turn the match with the help of two tie-breaks, 7-6, 7-6. The scores in the

tie-breaks 7-4 and 7-5, show how close the win had been.

I met another Czech in the second round, Vladimir Zednik, and had an easy win in two straight sets, 6-4, 6-0, but that was the end of the so-called easy matches and also the end of the public's one-sided and unreserved support of me as "the boy". In the quarter-finals, I came up against one of the USA's most popular players, the Davis Cup player and seed number three, Tom Gorman. It was a tremendously well-played and exciting match, which was even at the deciding set. I had won the first set by 6-4 and Gorman the second by 7-5.

Focus on victory
My play went fantastically well on the asphalt. I was geared completely to win, although we took it in turns to take each other's service games, so that the game position was 6-6 and the whole match was to be decided by a tie-break. My hopes were realised. Of the nine points in the tie-break, Gorman won only two. The set and match went to me, 7-6.

Now for the semi-final against Stan Smith, I thought as I left the Stadium after my well-deserved victory over Gorman. But on another court, the South African

In the USA I was also prey to the girls, but my American supporters behaved perfectly during the matches. Here with one of my fans, Suzan Marty, at a tournament in Oakland

53

Roy Emerson was too much for me in the final in Alamo. Here the Australian has received the first prize while I, for my second place, have received a somewhat smaller trophy. *Extreme right*, Jack Kramer.

Ray Moore's sensational win against Stan Smith had happened, and I am not exaggerating when I say that at that change of scene, my chances of winning were increased by at least thirty per cent. The court was packed with about five thousand spectators when Ray Moore and I began competing for a place in the finals in the Fireman's Fund Tournament and again the crowd had come to express its sympathy

for "the young Swede".

No threat
In an hour, I had fulfilled the spectators' hopes, winning by 6-3, 6-3, without even feeling threatened. Moore could not find his form against my swift and rapid play and I was able to dominate the match both from the base line and at the net. I returned better, a fact that decided the match.

My name now ranked higher than ever before during my stay in the USA, and at the Tennis Stadium the atmosphere was reminiscent of what I had experienced at Wimbledon a few months earlier. At the entrances, they were selling large badges with my portrait on them, and they were clearly doing very well, as my young women supporters were queuing to buy them.

I was living with an American family a few hundred yards away from the Stadium during that tournament, and outside the Stadium and my temporary home there were always about thirty or forty girls faithfully waiting for me. In contrast to Wimbledon's girls, the American girls supported me with perfect behaviour during the matches, no comments, not a sound, until the point had been played. Then came the applause, or, if I lost the point, deep sighs of compassion.

Apart from the result of the final against Roy Emerson, I was satisfied with this tournament, which I regarded as my best hitherto. Once again I found myself in the position of having nothing to lose and everything to gain, though perhaps it was a feeling I was to experience for the last time against Roy Emerson. There was so little between me and victory in this final, perhaps a decimetre.

At 4-4 in the deciding set, I had one point to go to win the game. In that situation I hit an easy ball about a decimetre outside the court, probably deciding the match. I was out of rhythm after that, lost the game and the next one. The final went to Emerson 5-7, 6-1, 6-4.

15. Becoming a millionaire

The quarter-finals in the Canadian Championships produced 8,000 kronor (£800) and my place in the American Championships meant that I could add a further 5,000 kronor (£500) to my bank account. Altogether I had earned 200,000 kronor (£20,000) in 1972 and 1973, and even if I don't exactly keep acounts of income and expenditure, one of the driving forces of tennis is the amazing amount of money one can earn at it.

In some tournaments, the final prize can amount to 250,000 to 300,000 kronor (£25-30,000), and players like Rod Laver, Ilie Nastase, Roy Emerson, Stan Smith and Arthur Ashe have long been millionaires from their sport. I could not accept prize money until the International Tennis Association abolished the eighteen-year-old age-limit – a decision that was not taken until I was seventeen.

Money to the Association

Before that, my income from tennis had gone straight to the Swedish Tennis Association, my previous employer. Amongst other things, the money was transformed into air flights, hotel rooms and pocket money. I never had to pay for anything myself and to be honest, I have never *lost* on my arrangement with the Tennis Association.

Tennis has become more and more commercialized, not least in the USA, where television companies fight over the big professional tournaments, and perhaps it is a matter of time before the tennis professionals begin to insist that longer interviews are only granted on condition that television, radio and newspaper rights are included.

I do not know what is right and what is wrong in this case. Naturally, tennis players feel a certain responsibility towards the mass media, who year after year turn the spotlights on the sport, but on the other hand, one cannot get away from the fact that these interviews take up an enormous amount of a player's time. I have always had very good relations with tennis journalists and have never asked for fees for an interview, but after talking to twenty journalists in one and the same day, I must admit that my irritation is great when the twenty-first appears.

The same questions

Normally the same questions are asked and sometimes one would prefer to sneak away from it all to some safe hiding-place. It has happened occasionally after a lost match that I haven't placed myself at the disposal of the press at exactly the moment the press had expected, but on those occasions I have swiftly patched up our good relations. No

My mother pastes into cuttings-books
everything that is written about me.
It's quite a lot

the article is taken up as a general topic of conversation. I nearly always surprise them by saying that I haven't seen it and that I rarely read the newspapers.

Comics

I exclude the strip-cartoon papers that travel round with me in my cases, together with my tennis equipment and tape-recorder, when I pack for another tournament. I cannot explain my lack of interest in reading, but the fact is I have been just as uninterested in sports articles on myself as on other people ever since I started training regularly. At most, I look at the pictures and read the captions. Possibly I will acquire an appetite for reading articles when I've finished with competitive tennis and my mother hands over the cutting-books which cover my tennis life tournament by tournament. But that is not certain.

I very seldom watch television, or listen to the radio, to hear a Björn Borg interview. On the other hand, I always hurry home when a taped broadcast of a match I have played in is being televised. Then I concentrate wholly on the play and on myself on the screen. The picture mercilessly reveals all my faults and failings, and I have often learnt as much from the televising of a match as I have from long training sessions on the court.

player wants to risk being regarded as a prima donna and I myself have always reacted strongly against every tendency to such behaviour, while at the same time I am aware that no one can go round being pleasant all the time.

Often when I meet a journalist, he or she asks whether I have read this or that article, sometimes an article which has triggered off the meeting with me. There are times when

16. Stockholm — dream and nightmare

Stockholm Open was both a dream and a nightmare. It was a dream come true when I reached the final in a packed Stadium, before an expectant home crowd, and with television broadcasting my luckiest tournament. I write "luckiest" instead of "best", because to tell the truth, I did not play *especially well* in the Royal Hall. On the other hand, I have never fought so successfully, gained so much from the inspiration the crowd offered, or received such a large share of decisive points. In match after match, it was will-power that saved me.

After my defeat in the final against Tom Gorman, I was often told that I had been only a couple of points away from another 19,000 kronor (£1,900) – the second prize earned me 26,000 (£2,600) – but at the time I was not calculating my income in kronor, but in what tennis had previously offered and what I now had to pay.

The great crisis

All through that autumn, I had been suffering from player's fatigue, and soon after the Stockholm Open, the great crisis arose. Directly after the final match against Tom Gorman, I packed my cases to go chasing after more Grand Prix points in Nottingham and London. The Grand Prix list revealed that I lay so well ahead in the top half of the list that with a reasonable end to the season – Nottingham, London and Buenos Aires – I would qualify for the Masters Tournament in Boston at the beginning of December. The Masters Tournament is the equivalent of the final for the Grand Prix, in which the eight best players on the list fight for about 250,000 kronor (£25,000).

It began promisingly with an easy victory against Manuel Orantes in Nottingham – my first win over him in five meetings – but then came the catastrophe against the Englishman, Mark Cox, in the second round. I left the court totally played out. However much I tried to concentrate, it had been impossible to dispel the thoughts that circled round the thousand things I had to do off the court.

Chasing Grand Prix points

Fortunately, I could now go straight home to Sweden and my parents in Södertälje. At first, I was supposed to be going on with my trainer, Lennart Bergelin, to Brussels and the King's Cup match against Belgium, but because the Tennis Association knew that at that time I was chasing valuable Grand Prix points, I was excused the

Left, My parents are my most faithful supporters and go to my matches whenever possible. Here *(encircled)* at the final of the Stockholm Open.

Above, I am thanking Gorman for a good match *(left)* and receiving a few words of consolation from King Carl-Gustaf *(right)*

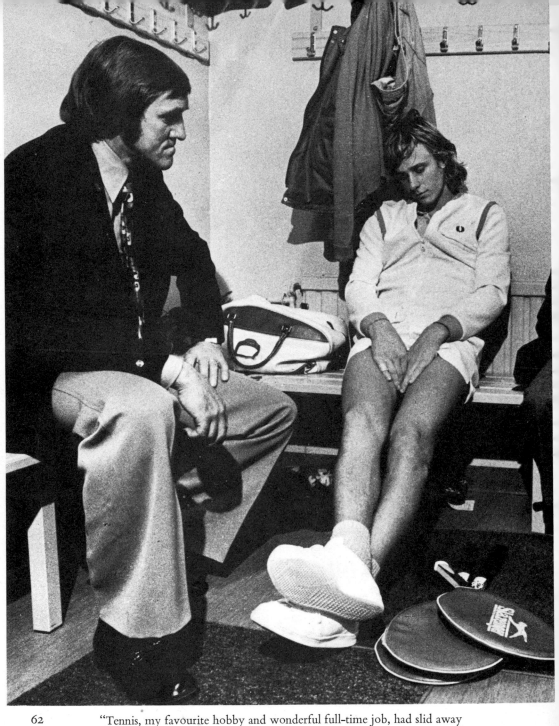

62   "Tennis, my favourite hobby and wonderful full-time job, had slid away from me". Here I am consoled by my trainer, Percy Rosberg

Belgium tournament.

But I was only at the beginning of my crisis. After my arrival at Södertälje, I fixed training sessions with my club trainer Percy Rosberg, in the SALK hall, as a last run through before my departure for Argentina and Buenos Aires, a trip which I made with Kjell Johansson.

After fifteen minutes knocking-up with Percy, I realised what a bad state I was in. Whatever I did, and I really did make an effort, I found it impossible to concentrate on my tennis, on the balls which Percy so patiently returned. I became more and more irritable trying to talk myself back, throwing my racket at the net and the side nets, hurling balls at the walls and ceiling out of sheer rage, and finally my irritation turned into fear.

Face in my hands

After fifteen minutes of this, I gathered up my rackets, left the court, sat down on a bench in the dressing-room, buried my face in my hands and felt relief at being able to cry it out. Percy, who was sitting beside me, did his best to console me, and said:

"Björn, harmony is the most important thing. Tennis life isn't worth much when you are hostile to the actual game."

That's exactly what it was. Tennis had slid away from me. In a few moments, everything became clear – the chase after tournaments, points and money and the general public's chase after Björn Borg were about to break me; an intolerable position which I managed to extricate myself from, and which in future I would avoid by planning things better.

I don't know exactly how many tournaments and matches I played in in 1973, probably something like at least one match every other day, and added to that the journeys, training and other preparations. From 1974 onwards, I was to cut down the number of competitions by at least twenty per cent and hope that my membership of the tennis professionals' trades union (ATP) would mean that I could hive off a great deal of my so-called administrative tasks.

A normal talent

How good a tennis player could I become? That depended entirely on myself. I like to think I have a normal talent and will not stop developing because of lack of aptitude. If I went on training and overcame the inevitable attacks of boredom, then I could become a really good player. But a great deal could happen in a negative direction during the coming years. I imagine that seventeen to twenty-one is the most sensitive period of a person's life, and I take absolutely nothing for granted.

Five years hence

In five years' time I will have all the answers, when I am twenty-two and the "trial period" is over. If I am not taking part in the fight for the finals in the big tournaments in five years' time, that will be the end of competitive tennis for me and I shall turn my whole attention to another profession.

In that case, I place my hopes in SAS and further training with them. I shall never go back to school, although I have no grades from my last year in all but three subjects.

17. "Or else he's crazy..."

The 1974 season could not have started better, as twice it was vouchsafed that I was now among the best sixteen players in the world.

First I was invited to take part in the great television tournament, CBS Classic, in Texas, USA, a knock-out tournament, behind closed doors, which during the following months was to be serialized to the American television public. Sixteen players took part in the tournament, "the best and most attractive players in the world", as it said on the invitation.

There was only a week until the WCT premiere in Philadelphia and after that tournament, I saw ahead such a compressed programme that there would be room for nothing else but tennis and travelling. The alternative to the CBS Classic was a lightning visit to my parents at home in Södertälje, and I did not hesitate.

Then came the seeding in Philadelphia. In the 1973 merits, the computers spat me out as the sixteenth best player in the world; seeded in the season's first WCT tournament – the professionals' unofficial world championship – with 450,000 kronor (£45,000) in the kitty and 70,000 kronor (£7,000) to the winner of the singles class! Unfortunately I could not thank them for their confidence in me in the way I had

anticipated. My form had been somewhat up and down during recent months and this was reflected in my results.

My first competition, after a narrow defeat by Tom Gorman in the Stockholm Open, was a Grand Prix tournament in Buenos Aires, where I was forced to give up after an injury – two points from victory – against Guillermo Vilas in the final. More about that injury later.

Then I was knocked out of a tournament in Sydney, against the Englishman, Mark Farrell, and lost against the eventual finalist, Phil Dent, in Melbourne.

The Australian and New Zealand tour ended happily after all, as in Auckland I won the singles after an almost faultless match on grass against Onny Parun (3-0).

From Philadelphia to the Albert Hall

The first match in Philadelphia was not at all as I expected. A walkover against the Czech Jiri Hrebec perhaps sounds nice and easy, but it turned out that I was faced with three difficult sets against Tony Roche of Australia in the second round. Roche won by 7-6, 7-6, and to lose so narrowly – 4-7 and 6-7 at tie-break, plus a missed set-point in each set – is one of the worst things that can happen.

It was a defeat which stung, and not until

I made my first bull's eye in WCT – in the Albert Hall in London a month later – did my disappointment disappear. I very much wanted to match up to the high opinion the WCT organisers had of me, and one February evening, in my third WCT tournament, I had a chance to show at least one thing – I hadn't lost to Tony Roche from nervousness.

The whole of the WCT tournament in the Albert Hall constitutes a number of pleasant memories for me. But I will skip the "pre-matches" and go straight on to the final against the Englishman, Mark Cox, because I have never been in such a poor position and yet managed to turn a defeat into victory.

Cox won the first set 7-6 and was leading 5-3 and 40-love when I began my incredible recovery. After three saved match points, we drew at 6-6. At tie-break, Cox led 6-4 and so had two more match points. Again I managed to reduce his lead, rose to 6-6 and landed in a situation in which Cox had game, set and match point – at the same time as I had game and set point.

I remember how I rushed up to the net and once again managed to take an untakeable shot. 7-6 in both sets and tie-break and the match was wide open for the deciding set. My six saved match points clearly made an impression on the crowd in that venerable hall. Earlier on in the match, I had had the schoolgirls on my side. After my recovery to 1-1, I received applause from the dinner-jacketed gentlemen in the boxes as well. In the hall packed with 6,000 people, there were suddenly *two* favourites.

In the deciding set, we kept each other company up to 4-4 and then I broke Cox's service and took my own service game 6-4. The Albert Hall was like a boiling cauldron after the final. People stood in the seats and sang, shouted, whistled and clapped when I left the court – an atmosphere which reminded me very much of the Royal Hall and Stockholm Open three months earlier. And yet that was only the beginning of the evening in the Albert Hall.

Two hours later Ove Bengtson and I were the winning finalists in the doubles against the English pair, John Lloyd and Mark Farrell, 7-6, 6-4. After the singles final, Mark Cox said to the Swedish and English journalists:

"Borg is either extremely brave and has no nerves – or else he is crazy. I've never in all my tennis career seen a player hit such daring stop-balls at the end of a big final!"

I countered with the explanation that one never wins a match without taking risks. "And you know I never give up . . . !"

Perhaps I ought to have added that in fact I didn't believe I'd win after Cox twice having three match points. The truth is that I just clipped at the ball and hoped it would fall on the right side of the net and lines. Six times my hopes were fulfilled and the single and double finals together meant I received my hitherto largest prize, 50,000 kronor (£1,000).

18. Bergelin taught me to live

The only people left in that finals evening which had been so successful for Ove Bengtson and me were a few players in my green WCT group. Players who are knocked out in the first, second and third rounds rapidly fly off to their next destination to get acclimatised and to familiarise themselves with courts and their surroundings. It is very rare for a player to win two tournaments running, so I arrived in Spain and Barcelona with no other thought than of surviving a couple of rounds after my successes in London.

However, I remember some truths I had learnt from my daily tennis-life – from our national coach, Lennart Bergelin – and although I was tired out, I had far from given up hope in advance. Bergelin always says over and over again to his boys:

first, play tennis; secondly, eat well; thirdly, live cheaply.

I now lived my professional life exactly according to those maxims.

The biggest advantage of living simply – preferably at a small obscure hotel – is that I can quickly get to know the porter. He is usually in a position at the hotel where he is both the hall porter and in charge of the switchboard. People ring me up from all over the world and it is nice to hear my friend the hall porter saying: "Björn Borg stayed here for a few days but has now moved to another hotel."

What if my parents want me on an important matter? We have arranged that I ring them up in Monte Carlo two or three times a week. But more about my move to Monaco later.

Training with Lennart Bergelin

19. Laver gets two games

All tennis players sooner or later are asked the question: "Which was your best match ever?" Many can probably answer within a few seconds. Others, and I am one of them, need plenty of time to think. On the other hand, I can at once say which first-class match had the best set-score and took the minimum of time: the WCT match against Rod Laver of Australia, in Barcelona on February 28th, 1974.

In forty minutes, I defeated Laver 6-1, 6-1.

When did I feel victory was mine? Not until the score was 5-1 in the second set. Perhaps that sounds cautious in the extreme, but I have seen Laver make such incredible recoveries that I was on my toes right up to match point.

Laver seemed stiff and slow and never really got the feel of the ball in this match. And I did not envy him at the start. He had not much to gain by beating me, but a great deal to lose.

When we left the court after the match, Laver said:

"Well played, Björn."

Laver is known for his taciturnity, but when he says something, he means every word. I had played a good match and the Spanish newspapers were overwhelming with their praise the next day.

Laver and I have met and played against each other many times since that sensational match in Barcelona, but he has never even commented on it. But from an American journalist, I heard that Laver said at a press conference in Houston a few months later:

"The match in Barcelona? I've forgotten the scores."

Laver has probably persuaded himself that that match does not count, that it is forgotten, and in that I have learnt yet another thing from him; forget bitter defeats and look ahead. It's best for you that way . . .

My best match?

There are seven, in no particular order:

Adriano Panatta, 3-1, Båstad Grand Prix
Ken Rosewall, 2-1 in Toronto
Onny Parun, 3-0 in Auckland
Rod Laver, 2-0 in Barcelona
Arthur Ashe, 3-0 in Dallas
Ilie Nastase, 3-0 in Rome
Tom Okker, 3-0 in Boston.

Please note that I have put down my best *technically played* matches. If best means the matches in which I have turned defeat into victory through will and fighting spirit, none of the above matches would be in my top ten list.

With my good friends Tom Okker and Arthur Ashe in Barcelona

Here I am surrounded by journalists in Spain

20. My thumb insured

How long can Björn Borg last?

Ever since I took the big step into the world tennis élite, people have been asking that question. The reason why? Perhaps, as opposed to many other players, because I admit to being tired after a long match and a long tournament. Perhaps because my playing style looks such hard work; and it *is* quite tiring.

I have only once been worried about my future, and that was when I had to be helped off the court during my finals match against Guillermo Vilas in Buenos Aires in 1973.

As I was chasing a ball, I fell so awkwardly on to an umpire's chair that I injured my back and was forced to give up. The newspaper headlines next day were exactly what I suspected:

"Borg – knocked out by a chair!"

After that accident, I was forced to give up both training and matches, so had plenty of time to discuss the risk of injuries with my parents. This family discussion led to my taking out a special insurance which among other things included that the loss of a thumb was the equivalent of total disablement. My future hangs first and foremost on my being fit and avoiding injuries. I am also insured against lengthy illness.

After practically every tournament, I was showered with warnings. Arthur Ashe and Rod Laver both pointed out the danger of playing too much. "You'll kill your talent, Björn". It has even gone so far that a physiologist and condition-trainer at GIH (College of Physical Education) in Stockholm quite seriously suggested that within a short time I would suffer from what they called a professional injury, an injured back caused by too one-sided and heavy strain, because I did not do enough gymnastics and exercises etc.

I realise that all this advice is well-meaning, but there is no real reason why I should change my training programme, is there? A thorough medical report, in connection with my call-up for military service, revealed that I was completely fit, that my scores were *very* good and my pulse at rest 35, which is said to be something of a record for Swedish athletes.

I have also been told that my running technique is bad, but as far as I can remember I would not have hit half so many balls over the net if I had been supple and had a beautiful running technique. Apart from the injury in Buenos Aires, I have had no trouble with my back, only occasional stiffness, and every tennis player has that.

21. Only human

During a spell in the spring of 1974, I could count seventeen singles matches without a defeat. My form had been stable for quite a while, my success so great that it came as a shock for many when I suddenly crashed. It was, however, a reaction and a defeat – against the stateless, previously Czech, Milan Holecek, at Nottingham Grand Prix – that I took with a smile. I was both physically and mentally exhausted, and thus more in need of a rest than further tournament successes or prize money.

So I was disappointed at the reaction to defeat number two – which came a few weeks later in the match against the Egyptian, Ismali El Shafei, at Wimbledon. The English newspaper, the *Daily Express* gave some of the country's most well-known sportsmen the opportunity to comment on my Wimbledon contribution, which apart from the defeat against El Shafei, consisted of a clear victory over the Englishman, Graham Stilwell, and an almost equally watertight win against Australia's Ross Case. The latter match was much commented on, as I protested against it not being postponed because of bad light.

Here are some comments from the *Daily Express*:

Lester Piggott, England's leading jockey:

"Björn Borg must learn better self-discipline. Discipline and temperament are the A to Z of a star player."

Alan Pascoe, international 400 metres sprinter: "Björn Borg likes publicity far too much, and this can become his downfall. He constantly complained that he was too tired and yet one could not switch on the radio or television during Wimbledon without hearing or seeing him. He seems to have any amount of time for that."

Dennis Amiss, leading cricketer: "Björn Borg complained of mental fatigue. If one cannot keep that in check, it is meaningless to play at top level. As soon as one's concentration has gone, one becomes worthless in precision sport."

I have often been asked whether I regret that outburst of anger in the match against Ross Case. No, the tennis public must sooner or later learn that I am not a kind of hitting-machine, but an ordinary person. At Wimbledon in 1974, I was surrounded by a halo which benefited neither my tennis nor me. Worst were the accusations that I liked publicity. I, who go long roundabout ways to avoid interviews, but who have learnt to appear at press conferences so as not to sabotage the jobs of hundreds of journalists!

22. The WTT series

In the autumn of 1973, it became clear that I could no longer manage all the business attached to tennis by myself, at the same time doing my best at training and tournaments. It was a matter of finding an agent, manager and financial adviser as quickly as possible, who would look after all advertising offers and commercial matters.

That man became the American, Mark McCormack, the same person who looks after the affairs of, amongst others, Jackie Stewart, Emerson Fittipaldi, Pelé, Jean-Claude Killy, Rod Laver, and Arnold Palmer. My connection with McCormack was not more than a few months old when a really big business deal lay before me – a contract with the American tennis league, World Team Tennis (WTT). The sum offered remains a secret between WTT, my possible WTT club in Cleveland, Ohio, McCormack and myself, but I am able to reveal that it was a gilt-edged offer and for a long time it was ninety per cent certain that I would sign. McCormack had checked up on everything and we were largely in agreement with Cleveland on the transfer fee.

WTT?

I admit that we tennis players regarded the league as more of a circus than pure sport; just one thing like WTT bringing in new rules, 1-0 instead of 15-love after a point won, and the first to get four wins the game, plus a number of other revolutionary changes. For as long as possible, I held Cleveland and the WTT organisers at bay and delayed signing. Meanwhile advice poured in to Tokyo, Houston and Denver, where my green WCT group was during the negotiations. Officials, players and good friends advised me in both directions, and I was in daily telephone contact with Sweden and the Swedish Tennis Association.

Before the decision was made, I had met up with Lennart Bergelin in Denver, and even if he did not in any way try to influence my decision, his appearance in the middle of Davis Cup preparations was evidence of how much they at home in Sweden wished to "keep" me. The feeling of being appreciated is always pleasant, and when at the very last moment I received a substantial counter-offer from the Swedish Tennis Association and a number of other tennis organisers in Sweden, McCormack could close the WTT negotiations. The trial of nerves was over and to Bergelin, I could for the first time admit that uncertainty over the future was beginning to drive me crazy. I could not sleep for worrying and had nothing to offer at my daily training.

Now at last I could transfer my concentration from contracts, money and tennis to nothing but tennis, and I was pleased to be able to continue what I think is the greatest fun on earth – the Davis Cup, competitions in Båstad and Stockholm, and the big tournaments in Europe. But it was certainly remarkable how swiftly the picture of the future changed my character.

23. The fans in Montreal

A week after turning down the WTT offer, I had reached the last but one stop in a four-month tour with another so-called circus: WCT and the doubles finals in Montreal. My memories of this visit are primarily hysterical idolizing which surpassed anything I had ever experienced in London and Wimbledon.

A few days before the tournament, we sixteen doubles-players were invited to what the organisers called on the invitation card "a small cocktail party". I had no idea that several hundred especially chosen guests – society ladies and notables – had been issued with quite a different kind of invitation card, on which they were bidden to "meet the players" – and were asked to wear long dresses and dinner jackets.

The party took place in a room in a hotel taken straight from the Arabian Nights and costing for the suite alone 20,000 kronor (£2,000) for the evening. The organisers had taken both the suite and the bar that night. I don't know whether anyone was offended – I don't think so – but as far as I could see, I was the only person there wearing an open-necked shirt and no tie. After drinks in the bar, there was no longer any reason to worry about ties. With or without a tie, I was now to the city's society

ladies just Björn Borg, the young tennis player and everyone's prey.

An example:

A beauty of thirty years ago – the average age was about sixty – wriggled forward, flashed her green eyelids and said:

"Give me a kiss, Björn."

Although I had Lennart Bergelin at my side, I felt a certain hesitation in face of such a request, which the lady made lightning use of:

"Come closer, Björn. That's right, that's right . . ."

Incidentally, I am never called Björn abroad; the dots over the o vanish and all that is left is Bjorn.

When Bergelin and I went into supper in the party suite, it turned out that the players had been honoured with a table apiece. Mine had places for fourteen people and eleven places were already taken up by members of my devoted fan club!

After the first glass of red wine, the ladies' "I like you, Björn" was no longer valid. Now I was *loved* by everyone, and sitting in the middle of this drum-fire of sugary phrases was a pleasure, as long as my smile remained spontaneous. After an hour, it felt glued on, and I leant over towards Bergelin and whispered:

"What awful old witches, Labbe!"

The reply was nothing but a heartless laugh, but half an hour later, Bergelin rescued me:

"Come on now, boy," he said. "Let's get back to the hotel. Tomorrow things'll be better, as then we'll play tennis."

A change of doubles partner

It was not all that much better, as Ove Bengtson and I had the misfortune to meet the South African pair, Fred McMillan and Bob Hewitt, in our first match. McMillan and Hewitt were at the time the best doubles-players in the world and they defeated us 3-1 and eventually won the whole tournament.

After the doubles tournament in Montreal, Ove went back to Sweden and Davis Cup training – for the match against Poland in Båstad. Lennart Bergelin and I went on to Texas and Dallas, where I had qualified for the singles finals in WCT, together with the seven best players in the world.

Unfortunately, Ove and I parted as a doubles pair six months later. Our harmonious play together suddenly stopped functioning and after a few unnecessary defeats, we agreed to part company. On my side, this meant that from 1975 onwards, I had Guillermo Vilas from Argentina as my doubles partner in WCT.

My most famous stroke: the double-handed backhand

24. WCT finals in Dallas

Texas and Dallas at the beginning of May, 1974.

This was something quite different from Montreal a week earlier, when icy winds had swept along the boulevards and round corners, enforcing a rather dreary indoor existence in hotel rooms and tennis halls. And taxis. Trips back and forth between two of the fixed points in my life.

As soon as I got off the plane at the gigantic airport at Dallas – the largest in area in the world – I was in a good mood. The warm air seemed to caress me and I felt a sense of contentment which I knew would influence my tennis game very positively. I love the heat and swimming, and here the WCT organisers were offering a constant air-temperature of 30-35 degrees Centigrade, plus a swimming-pool alongside the players' hotel.

A garden party at the home of Lamar Hunt the oil millionaire and a WCT director, is also one of the memories of a lifetime Lennart Bergelin and I took away with us from Dallas. Together with Bergelin and other players – John Newcombe, Stan Smith, Arthur Ashe, Rod Laver, Ilie Nastase, Jan Kodes and Tom Okker – plus journalists, photographers and all Lamar Hunt's millionaire friends, I found myself in a garden which as far as size was concerned outclassed Gröna Lund and Skansen Park combined. The Hunt family's natural friendliness, their ambition to arrange something extra for the players, is one of my memories which will never fade. During my brief career as a tennis player, I have met many people with a great deal of money, but seldom have I met a financier and millionaire who was so everyday and egalitarian as the tennis enthusiast, Lamar Hunt.

My tennis form?

Bergelin said just before we left Hunt's party at about nine that evening:

"The boy is thoroughly rested, plays well in training and is keen on tennis again. Anything can happen during these three days. Björn may be beaten in the first match. But he may also win the whole tournament."

The match with Ashe

I felt much like this. My appetite for the ball was back after the fatiguing WTT negotiations in Denver, and I was looking forward to my first match. I had had good luck in the draw, though there was not really a draw, as the players' placing and points in respective WCT groups decided the order of play. But even so, I had had

74

luck. Arthur Ashe, in the first match, Ashe, whom I had defeated twice in three matches in recent months.

First and foremost, it is the honour that matters in this tournament, regarded unofficially as the professionals' world championship. But the prize money is not to be sneezed at either: 230,000 kronor (£23,000) for the winner, 90,000 kronor (£9,000) to the losing finalist, and 40,000 kronor (£4,000) for a third place etc.

On my previous meetings with Ashe, I could not help noticing his popularity. When Ashe plays at home in the USA, the word popular is not sufficient to describe the relationship between him and the crowd. In Dallas, their relationship would be better described as idol-worship. Ashe was greeted with enormous jubilation when he was introduced and for the first time for a long time, I felt "my seventeen years" were not sufficient to obtain the majority of the spectators' sympathies.

I think I can say it was a match to the crowd's taste, perhaps even the best in the tournament. I will never forget one set of particularly good tennis, but allow me to skip both the first and the second – which I won 7-5, 6-4, as the third set and its ending demand a detailed description.

Ashe and I had reached 6-6 in games, when he began to serve at tiebreak, at first to seven winning points. In a few minutes, Ashe had collected an apparently secure 4-0 lead, when my service and my returns again began to function, 4-4. Then another following wind for Ashe, which made the score 5-4 and 6-5, and thus set-point, when again I recovered. 6-6 at tie-break in the third set, meant set point for both, that the

match was still wide open if Ashe won the next point and thus the third set, but that I HAD WON THE WHOLE MATCH IF I MANAGED TO TAKE ASHE'S SERVICE!

The Hitchcock direction of this match had now reduced the 10,000 spectators to a breathless silence and I was aware of the dull thud as Ashe bounced the ball on the floor before he hit his devastating first service.

Nervous?

No, remarkably enough, I wasn't a bit nervous. True, I was aware that this chance would never come again, but I certainly wasn't nervous. Then that first service came toward me. A short, twisting ball which landed in the service square on my backhand, Ashe simultaneously rushing up to the net to cover my return. I took a couple of steps to the side, waved with my two-handed backhand and saw Ashe in vain stretching out for my short, angled and chopped – well, call it a lucky shot – which fell just inside the line.

7-6 at tie-break and 7-6 in sets. The match was mine and the crowd too, in fact. The spectators stood in their seats and clapped and shouted, and indeed Ashe and I had offered good and exciting tennis. Indoor tennis of international class, as the papers said next day.

But one is not the winner on one win only, and in the next round, Jan Kodes was waiting after his sensational win over Ilie Nastase in the first round. After the match against Ashe, I was asked at a press conference whether I had met Kodes before.

"Yes, twice. Lost both times. But now I feel on fine form and can take my revenge."

Another question:

"Can you win the whole tournament?"

"Wait and see, gentlemen."

The match with Kodes

Perhaps this was not so well played or as dramatic as my first match. Kodes soon discovered that my backhand wasn't working and the consequent hammering at my weak point won him the first set, 6-4. In some way, I had to find a counter-weapon and as so many times before, it was my legs that saved me. I simply ran round the ball and hit forehand and with those tactics won that important set, 6-4. In the third set, I got back my backhand and after another 6-3 set win, and a clear 3-0 lead in the fourth, Kodes more or less gave up and let me finish comfortably at 6-2.

Before the final against John Newcombe, I had two days' much needed rest. After the match against Kodes, my whole body ached, and if I was to have a chance against Newcombe, I had to make the most of every hour – yes, every minute – to rest. I got my rest, but I was not left in peace. Perhaps that was too much to ask, as I was a part of a "World Championship final" which interested the whole tennis world. I was told that the final was to be seen on television by about 400 million people, so against that background it is understandable that there was one press conference after another to give the public and television viewers all the pre-match information.

I especially remember one press conference at which both Newcombe and I were present and were being questioned. After a while, Newcombe said:

"Why did you ask me to come here, when you're only interested in Björn Borg?"

This is roughly the kind of question I got, and answer I gave:

"They say that half Sweden sits up listening to the radio when you play. In the middle of the night?"

"Not half Sweden, perhaps. But I know that Swedish Radio has a reporter here (Tommy Engstrand)."

"Do your parents sit up and listen too?"

"Yes, I rang them up after the match against Kodes and they were as pleased as I was. Pleased and surprised."

Theatrical whisper from John Newcombe: "I called up my *children* after my match against Stan Smith!"

"What about your tactics against Newcombe in the final?"

"I just go out and play. He serves so hard and has such fine volleys that I'll have to concentrate on getting the balls back."

"They say you left school in the ninth grade. Why?"

"Because I hated lessons and sitting inactive answering questions at a school desk."

"Many Swedish journalists are watching you here in Dallas. What do you feel about their presence?"

"In fact, I play better when they are sitting in the stands."

John Newcombe did not have nearly so many questions to answer. Everyone knew he was then the best player in the world, that he had won Wimbledon three times, the American Championships twice and the Italian and Australian Championships once and so on. My finals opponent was by far and away the favourite, in top form both physically and mentally, and at a party the evening before the match, I took the chance of ending my speech with a little appeal: ". . . and I'm only seventeen, John, so be nice to me tomorrow!"

The match with Newcombe

The final against Newcombe had a sensational introduction. All the experts were in agreement that I had a slight chance if I could win the first set. After fifteen minutes play, I was leading 5-1 in the first set. But Newcombe quickly recovered from his down-spell and took three games in a row before I had again shaken this great service and volley specialist to the extent of winning the set 6-4.

The continuation was not so sensational – or such fun. Let us say, I got to 2-0 in sets. Then Newcombe was forced to give everything in the third to survive the match – at the same time I could rest and devote myself to other diverse chances; rest before putting on a spurt, against a tiring Newcombe, in the fourth and/or fifth set. Lennart Bergelin also had a theory that I would have beaten John Newcombe if I had met him in my first match, when I was rested, fresh and keen to play. But then I would perhaps have come up against Ashe in the final and lost against him! I usually play best at the start of a tournament, which can probably be explained by the fact that my body is still growing and is not yet stabilized.

Finally a little picture of John Newcombe, who had not been given the opportunity to say much before the final, but who was all the more interesting after the match when the public demanded a victory speech from him. Newcombe took the microphone, thanked the organisers for a perfect competition,

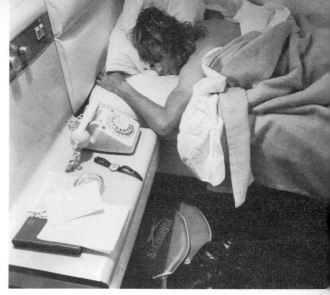

I enjoy a much-needed rest

commented on the four final sets and turned to me and said:

"You have here by my side the best seventeen year-old in the world, a world champion in two or three years. But, ladies and gentlemen, not just that. Björn Borg is the nicest guy I've ever met in my tennis career! I have a son (Clint Newcombe) who is five years old. I hope he will be just as good a sportsman as Björn Borg. I really do."

I received 90,000 kronor (£9,000) for my final placing. Tired and happy, I chased on to Europe, Sweden, Båstad and the 1974 Davis Cup premiere against Poland.

"Thanks," said the WCT organisers, as I left the tournament arena. "Thanks for all you've given WCT and the crowd here in Dallas."

"Thanks to you, too," I said, "for everything."

An adventure was over, another due to begin.

25. The hero from Dallas

After thirty hours with no sleep, I arrived at Båstad to face Davis Cup training for the Poland match, and I was ready to sleep round the clock.

When I woke, my physical exhaustion remained. I had become a sort of hero for autograph-hunters, journalists and photographers, and my steps were constantly watched by hundreds of eyes. Normally, I can manage this, but this time I was forced to break off my training, ask the journalists for a few days "break", and I gradually succeeded in shifting my training from Båstad Tennis Stadium to a court outside Båstad.

Then came the first singles match against Poland and I immediately landed in a fairly unnecessary bad situation – 2-6, 6-2, 0-6, against Tadeusz Nowicki. Pause for ten minutes, a brief chat with Lennart Bergelin, my club trainer, Percy Rosberg, and my parents, and I went out and turned the defeat into a victory, 6-1, 6-1.

That is how it went on for match after match. I played badly, but did my duty, that is to say, I won, but after clear wins both against Poland and Holland, I then had to face the big battle against Italy in July, the Davis Cup which was to fill the stands and eventually involve a come-back for Sweden as one of the best tennis nations in the world.

Immediately after the Holland match, I flew to Rome and the Italian Championships – still chasing after my first big title. Should I have gone home to my parents and taken a holiday instead?

"No," I said at a press conference in Båstad. "I'm looking forward to Rome."

But it was not the city itself which was enticing me there. Again I felt a desire to take up the struggle with the world's best (shale) players, Manuel Orantes, Ilie Nastase, Guillermo Vilas, Jan Kodes . . .

26. The Italian Championships

The Italian Open Championships have long been regarded as one of the most famous tournaments in the world. Up to the 1970s, the Australian, French and American Championships and Wimbledon were the four main tournaments. Now the Italian Championships have replaced the Australian in the "big four".

Only two players have taken the "grand slam" – that is, won all four of the biggest tournaments in the same year: Donald Budge, USA, in 1938, and Rod Laver, Australia, in 1962 and 1969. Only two Swedish players have ever won any of the four (five) big tournaments: Sven Davidson in France in 1957, and Jan-Erik Lundkvist in Rome in 1964.

The matches with Dominquez, Orantes, Vilas and Nastase

I had absolutely no plans of going down in Swedish history when I went out on to the court for my first match – against the Frenchman, Patrice Dominquez (6-2, 7-5). True, I had been seeded number three after the previous year's champion Ilie Nastase, and Jan Kodes, but to reach the final of this wasps' nest of the world's best shale-players and on top of that *win* the final against Nastase over and above a long row of tiring matches, was an inaccessible target, not even worth setting up, for at this time, Nastase was considered almost unbeatable on shale.

Although my legs refused to obey my orders, and the results of the next matches became an affair between my will and my opponents' repertoire of strokes, I built on the series of victories at Båstad and the Davis Cup, and suddenly found myself in the quarter-finals against Spain's best player, Manuel Orantes.

A difficult match with a stimulating task. If when not on top form, I could win against a shale specialist like Orantes, then that would mean I had the stability required to offer Nastase at least reasonable opposition in a possible final . . .

Orantes played well. He almost never plays a bad match on shale, but this time it was not enough. I took revenge for three shale defeats and won fairly easily with 6-2, 7-5.

I met Guillermo Vilas in a semi-final which he and I still sit and talk about in hotel rooms all over the world today. When the match was stopped because of bad light, the position was 2-6, 3-6, 6-3, 6-4, 1-1. For three hours we had tortured each other in 40 degrees Centigrade of sizzling hot sun and even if I had had the energy to go on when the umpire stopped play – and then I would have probably taken the match in better condition – I was thankful to crawl into the shower and rest before going on. Before I left the stadium, the organisers announced that the match would be completed at eleven o'clock the next day, after which the winner would have two hours in which to shower, eat lunch, rest and knock-up before the final against Nastase.

I did beat Vilas and at about one o'clock the following day, I was lying on a bench, resting and planning tactics against the best player on shale in the world.

Soon I had decided on my strategy.

I would meet Nastase with his own weapons. From beginning to end – no matter what the picture of the match looked like and how the game and set scores divided themselves – nothing but attack was engraved on my mind in this, my first great final.

In less than two hours, the match was over. In three straight sets, 6–3, 6–4, 6–2, I had defeated the "unbeatable" Nastase and played tennis which at moments was better than I had ever managed before.

Volley, smash, service, lobs, stop-shots – everything worked. Yes, after some balls even I had to admit to myself that "you've never really played this well before, have you, Björn? Really . . ."

All that remained then was that obligatory question – a few hours after the match. "How *good* had I been and how *bad* Nastase?"

One of the Swedes in the Rome stands, an ex-Davis Cup player, Thomas Hallberg, said this:

"For me, the match and your play were the best I've ever seen."

I had had a good finals day in the heat of Rome's tennis stadium. I also had a good finals evening. After the victory, I went with Thomas Hallberg and had dinner at a small restaurant, after which I went to bed very early, to give myself a much needed rest.

In other respects, I could not celebrate my greatest triumph, as instead of travelling direct to the French Championships in Paris, I went round via Stockholm and Södertälje to celebrate my eighteenth birthday, June 6th, at home with my parents.

Celebrating my eighteenth birthday with my parents

27. The French Championships

My diversion to see my parents looked like being to my cost at the French Championships in Paris. As seed number three, I arrived at my first match an hour before the announced time, and went direct from the airport to the Roland Garros stadium in a taxi, together with my tennis rackets, baggage and all my hand luggage.

My opponent in the first round was the Frenchman, Jean-Francois Caujolle, a player who had just qualified for the tournament and ranked number sixteen in France. I was aware that one should not come to a big tournament so ill-prepared – the French Championships still count as the World Championships on shale – but on the other hand, I have my eighteenth birthday only once in a lifetime, and so I thought it was worth the chance. "If it wrecks it all, well it'll have to . . ."

It nearly did. Caujolle took the first set 6-4, I the next 6-0, and in the third and deciding set Caujolle was 4-4 and 40-love with his own service. I had a stroke of luck then, which turned the match into a win with 6-4. But without some luck, one does not, of course, win any matches – that's a truth all through tennis.

Back to the hotel, unpack, make myself at home and prepare – really prepare – for the next match.

The Romanian, Toma Ovici, did not give me much trouble in the second round (2-0) and the next match went as easily – against the Frenchman, Jean Loup Rouyer (3-0) – and then the tournament went over from three- to five-set matches.

After the third round, however, the so-called easy opponents have usually gone from most tournaments, and the French Championships were no exception. In the last sixteen, Erik van Dillen was waiting, a swift and technical American who is dangerous to any player, with his bullet-like service and attacking volley-play, and although I had now won thirteen singles matches in a row since my finals defeat against John Newcombe, I was far from certain of victory.

Erik van Dillen fully succeeded with his attacking game of chance in the first set, 6-0, without my getting anywhere near a set-point. But how long would the American's chancy tennis last?

It lasted for a while in the second set – then it broke. After the third set, I had a firm grasp on the match from the moment I had turned 0-1 into 2-1. In the last and deciding set, there was almost a crisis. I was leading by 4-3, but van Dillen had 40-30, and in a weak moment, I had time to think: "If he takes this point and gets 4-4, anything could happen."

However, I won this psychological game, and five minutes later the whole match was mine after 6-3.

The quarter-final

I had reached the quarter-final and now the timetabling of every hour of the day was as important as actual initiative on the court. At about nine in the morning, I set off for the Roland Garros Stadium, trained, and played matches. In the doubles with the Russian, Alex Metreveli, I reached the semi-finals, and I also checked on future opponents from the stands. I did not usually return to the hotel until about eight in the evening.

Time for the quarter-final against Raul Ramirez of Mexico. Another tough five sets, 6-4 in the deciding set. Some tennis prophet once said that all training is easy after a win – that one should not then feel tired from the day before – and for a long time I have agreed that that observation is true. During the long tournaments in Rome and Paris, I discovered however, that no victories are so great that they can obliterate the effects of the sun and heat during a three hour match.

The semi-final

Faced with the semi-final against Harold Solomon, USA, I felt the match against Ramirez in my legs, and I knew what was to be expected: another long nightmare in 40 degrees Centigrade. I knew this not least from the fact that Solomon had exhausted Nastase in a long five-set match the day before and his tactics against me would be the same.

I used another tactic, keeping the ball in play and varying the length, forcing Solomon into the corners occasionally, and then rushing up to the net. Solomon revealed afterwards that he had cramp in both legs in the last set, and I myself had a slight touch of cramp in the first set.

After my win against Solomon, I collapsed on to a bench in the massage room and for the next half an hour experienced the indescribable feeling of pleasure as the masseur softened up my stiff muscles and cleaned up the mess of callouses, crooked toe-nails and sore feet.

"How can you play with feet like that?" said a journalist walking past.

"My feet?" I said. "My feet are my weapons of victory!"

Without massage, I would never have been able to give Manuel Orantes a match in the final. Anyhow, perhaps it was just as well I had my sore feet and tired body to bother about and concentrate on. Then I did not start thinking about what lay ahead – the fact that I now had a chance of winning *both* the Italian and the French Championships within a period of three weeks. To be the first Swede to take two of tennis's really great titles! I had received a reminder of the solemnity of the moment in the changing-room after the match against Harold Solomon. Henry Cochet, 72 years old, came up and congratulated me on my finals place.

"Björn, you are one of the greatest fighters I've seen on the tennis court. Good luck to you, my lad, and go to bed early so that you can manage the final tomorrow."

Cochet won the French Championships five times – 1922, 1926, 1928, 1930 and

1932, and together with Jean Borotra and Rene Lacoste formed "the three musketeers."

Later that evening, I heard that Swedish Television had made some changes to their programmes and decided to broadcast the finals match between Manuel Orantes and me direct. So there *was* something special about this final and when I fell asleep that evening, I had promised myself and my faithful companion, Lennart Bergelin, to give everything in return.

Only once more. Then I was to be allowed to rest before Wimbledon.

The final

It was as I thought and feared: Orantes forced me to scrape the barrel of my physical resources, and that match will for ever remain the most exhausting I have ever played. Orantes won the first set with outclassing style, 6-2, playing tennis which only he is capable of in his best moments; straight and angled shots, dead straight passes, both on the backhand and forehand, and with a wonderful feel for when he is to use his lobs and stop-shots.

I had far from given up hope of victory, but said to myself: "Now you must get the second set at all costs, otherwise you're lost in this baking heat."

Nothing much worked for me in the second set, but I hit back every ball, and got as near to winning the set as I could with four missed set-points.

Orantes took the second set, too, but with 7-6 after tie-break, and if there was anyone left in Roland Garros Stadium who still believed in me, then not even I shared that opinion! This is what I said in the *Express*

afterwards:

"I realise that many people, perhaps the majority, identified me with a loser after I had lost the first set and then the second – despite all those set-points. To be quite honest, I thought I was going to lose after 0-2 in sets. But however gloomy it looks, however great a lead your opponent has, I never give up. Perhaps you know that. It is just that a tennis match is never over until the match-point has been won."

It really had been a fantastic match, not least because of the reaction of the crowd. The majority usually sympathise with the weaker player, and when I started my recovery after 2-0, it felt as if the Roland Garros Stadium had become one great big "home ground". The normally quiet and reserved French spectators suddenly began to behave like football fans in the stands. At every change of end, I was applauded for several minutes. 10,000 spectators stood up in their seats and that was not just because of the sticky heat and the need to cool their backsides!

It was playing "with the wind", the crowd with me, and in this stimulating atmosphere, I turned what was an apparently hopeless defeat into the win of my life: 2-6, 6-7, 6-0, 6-1, 6-1. Afterwards I asked Lennart Bergelin what he thought about the match.

"I can't say how happy I am," he said. "I've never seen such a fight. Sometimes it was more difficult to sit in the stands than to play."

For once, Lennart had answered by unreservedly doling out praise. Otherwise, he usually keeps cool, whoever I have beaten, and he doesn't exactly shower the superlatives around. He was definitely slightly moved on that eventful afternoon in Paris.

After the finals, I invited my closest friends to a victory dinner in the Eiffel Tower; shrimp cocktails, sole and beer. It was the first time for two weeks I had allowed myself the luxury of eating fish. Normally I keep up my condition with juicy steaks, vegetables and mineral water, but with the knowledge that I now did not have an important match until Wimbledon in a couple of weeks, I could eat fish with good conscience.

"Are you happy?"

Someone put that question at the press conference after the final.

"Yes," I said. "This is the happiest day of my life."

"But you never smile."

"It's only on the court that I'm serious," I countered, smiling. "Otherwise I can't concentrate on the game."

I receive the congratulations of one of the veteran "three musketeers"

28. Prima Donna

After my finals wins in Rome and Paris, Lennart Bergelin suggested that I should get away from tennis in some way, for a few days' relaxation before Wimbledon.

"Go to West Germany and watch a Swedish World Cup football match or two," he said. "That's just what you need at the moment. Go and see the players in the team and get to know quite a different environment."

I liked the idea at once, and if I had not had to play in a Grand Prix tournament in Nottingham the week before Wimbledon, the German trip would certainly have come off. Lennart Bergelin's idea had been taken to such lengths that he even had a private plane ready to take us both to West Germany. But then the project fell through, as I was playing in both the singles and doubles class at Nottingham, and I did not want to let down my doubles partner, Ove Bengtson. Anyhow, the following weeks would show that everything that happened immediately after Paris and the French Championships went against me, as far as Wimbledon was concerned.

When the German trip fell through, I was offered, through an English journalist, a rest and a place to train at a private club just outside London. When this offer reached me, I considered it almost as good an alternative as the World Cup, and accepted at once. Cold shower number two, however, was not far away. As he did not know about this private club, Lennart Bergelin had booked me into a club in Birmingham. OK, Birmingham would probably have been a fine place, if the actual club hadn't arranged a big international tournament at the time, and if the organisers had not told the crowd through their loudspeakers that the "Swedish and French Champion Björn Borg is coming tomorrow . . ."

Birmingham became much like London and Wimbledon the year before, teenage girls and autograph hunters everywhere. When I think back on events in Nottingham and Birmingham, the planning of the 1974 season has a touch of the ridiculous about it, although I did not exactly overstrain myself at the Nottingham Grand Prix. I was defeated by Milan Holocek in the first match and made an equally swift exit in the doubles – 0-2 against the West German pair, Karl Meiler and Jurgen Fassbender.

On one occasion in Birmingham, I said to a journalist that "I am so tired that I'd like to go to sleep and never wake up again". That is not the best state to be in a week before Wimbledon.

The fans again

The Wimbledon seeding

Before I left Nottingham, the ranking at Wimbledon was announced. John Newcombe came first before Nastase, then Jim Connors, Stan Smith, then me. This grading of the top level caused a great deal of comment, not least in Sweden, where the experts considered that I was now one of the best three players in the world. Now I was seeded number five, which meant that my half in the match-list included players like Arthur Ashe, Stan Smith, Ken Rosewall and John Newcombe. I had hoped to be seeded number three, so now it was a question of accepting this reverse in the right way and most of all taking one match at a time.

I arrive in London

On my arrival in London, the bookmakers were saying that the interest in Björn Borg in 1974 was just as great as it had been the year before. On the traditional list, Newcombe stood at three to one, Nastase at four, myself five and so on. But then, and this was something quite new, I had a list of my own: the odds were fourteen to one that I would be knocked out in the first round, ten to one in the second, seven to one in the third, and so on. So I could have earned quite a pretty penny, for instance, by putting £100 on being knocked out in the first round. All I needed to do would be to lose and collect £1,400! But I *ought* to survive the first round; I had beaten Graham Stilwell twice earlier on in the season, though not on grass.

My arrival in London was also noticed by the newspapers, radio and television. There was not a day during which I was not booked for interviews and I had hardly stepped inside the walls of Wimbledon before I was surrounded by three or four London bobbies. After Wimbledon, I was told that a circular letter had been sent out from the organisers to the heads of three hundred girls' schools in London, containing an appeal to their pupils to leave me alone! They said that "Wimbledon is not a pop concert", but the fact is that when I assemble all the schoolgirls' reactions at my matches, the result is definitely positive. Indeed, I had been irritated many a time, but their comments had also helped me overcome many crises and turn defeats into victories.

Recording for the BBC

I resort to desperate measures to escape the fans

Wimbledon 1974

I was given the honour of playing on the centre court and returned this confidence by winning against Stilwell 6-1, 4-6, 6-4, 6-1. But it was not a good match. My play was not working at all, and I realised things were going to be difficult.

My forebodings began to come true in the very next match.

My troubles were not on the whole those of form, but primarily external circumstances which caused what the British press the following day called "the scandal at Wimbledon".

It poured with rain when my next match was due to be played against Australia's Ross Case, and not until about five o'clock had

the blackest clouds dispersed and the tarpaulin covering the court been rolled up. Case won the first set 6-3, I the second 6-1, and, although Case had set point, I won the third, too, 8-6. At 2-1 to Case in the fourth set, a huge black cloud sailed over the courts and at change of ends, I appealed to the umpire to stop the match because of bad light. I simply couldn't see the ball, and Case complained of the same thing.

However, the umpire had his instructions and said:

"Continue play!"

I appealed to the senior umpire of the court, and after a brief discussion, the order was repeated:

"Continue play!"

I replied by collecting up my rackets, putting on my outer clothes and giving everyone, including Lennart Bergelin, the impression that I was about to leave the court. In actual fact, I was only interested in seeing what my threat would lead to and to be quite honest, I had no thought of giving up the match. The consequences of my demonstration, however, were that I came near to being disqualified for unsportsmanlike behaviour, and five minutes after the interruption, I was once again on the court.

The crowd had meanwhile reacted violently.

"Borg is a coward!" shouted a spectator. "It's just as dark for both of you. Go on playing!"

"Borg is right," came from another direction. "It's scandalous, a lottery playing tennis in this coal cellar . . ."

When the match started up again, I lost my first service and then returned – in pure rage, I must admit – Case's service far outside the court. A ball landed on the players' restaurant, thirty yards away. At 4-1 to Case in the fourth set, the umpire stopped play because of bad light, that is to say, only three or four minutes after my demonstration and protest; a touch of Wimbledon prestige.

The next day the rain continued to ruin the Wimbledon programme and while waiting to continue the match, I had plenty of time to think about the fierce criticism I had had in the Swedish press, too. My parents told me on the telephone that Sweden's largest morning paper, *Dagens Nyheter* called me a "spoilt prima donna" in giant headlines, and in the next they even said "spoilt, stupid prima donna", which hurt me profoundly.

I consider myself least of all a prima donna, and whatever my age, as a tennis player, I shall continue to protest against playing when I can no longer see the ball. Hitting a couple of balls out of court was perhaps a stupid thing to do, but on the other hand, no one wins at tennis without temperament. The fault this time was that I could not contain my anger inside me.

When the match against Ross Case finally took place between showers, my entrance was more like that of a heavy-weight champion boxer being escorted from the changing-room to the ring. Four bobbies had their work cut out getting me through the crowd. It was a match everyone wanted to see, but it was played on number two court which meant only about 3,000 spectators could get in. After ten minutes play, the match was again interrupted by rain for two hours, then ten more minutes play took the score from 1-4 to 7-5, and thus I moved on to the third round.

After the match against Case, Wimbledon's press conference room was filled with journalists and, amongst other things, I was asked:

"Wasn't it difficult to get going again after all that rain and waiting?"

I answered truthfully.

"No, I felt the support from the stands and that was just what I needed."

Some critics feared that my good relations with the Wimbledon crowd had come to an end after this incident, but the continuation of the match showed that I was still playing on "home-ground".

I met the Egyptian, Ismail El Shafei, in the third round, a match which perhaps will always be my most useful defeat. In an hour I was outclassed, the score to El Shafei 6-2, 6-3, 6-1, and I ought not to have collected such poor scores against a player of El Shafei's standard. Perhaps it looked as if I gave up at the beginning of the third set, but I did try, and the bitter truth is that I had nothing left to give.

Disappointed after my defeat?

No, neither pleased nor disappointed. I had been given something to think about in the future, and never again would I repeat the mistake of the summer of 1974. Mistake? That I had not skipped the French Championships after my success in Rome and the Italian Championships. True, I would then have missed that wonderful time in Paris, but to be able to do myself justice at Wimbledon, the world's most famous and traditional tournament, I would have to be quite rested and enormously keen to play.

In play against Ross Case at Wimbledon

The concentration that Wimbledon demands

29. My most difficult opponents

Tennis players are like boxers. The next day, after a bout, everything seems much better. After a few days with my parents in Sweden, my desire to play came back and the two weeks after Wimbledon culminated in the final against the Italian, Adriano Panatta, at Båstad's Grand Prix. My physical and mental well-being had returned to such an extent that I was able to offer the crowd my best match in Sweden, beating Panatta 6-3, 6-0, 6-7, 6-2.

A week later, I met Panatta again, this time in the Davis Cup. It was a pity that Italy's final victory was already assured before the last singles which included the meeting between Panatta and me. Lennart Bergelin said afterwards that he had never seen a better singles match at Båstad. I repeated my game from the Grand Prix final and again won 3-1.

Indianapolis, Boston and Forest Hills
The next big tournament was the American Open Championships on shale in Indianapolis.

If asked who would be my most difficult opponent during the coming years, at this time I would have given eight names: Jim Connors, Guillermo Vilas, Roscoe Tanner, Raul Ramirez, Harold Solomon (shale), Dick Stockton, Vijay Amritraj and Eddie Dibbs. Of these, I came up against two in the semi-finals and finals at Indianapolis, first Ramirez (7-5, 6-7, 6-4) and then Connors (7-5, 3-6, 4-6).

I very much wanted to win this final against the Wimbledon champion, Jim Connors, but it was evident that he mastered all kinds of surfaces, and personally I have no objections to his promotion to the "best tennis player of 1974".

I had hoped for revenge in Boston the following week, but then Connors clearly preferred to rest before the American shale championships at Forest Hills, New York – which he also won – as he vanished out of the tournament at an early stage. The competition in Boston, however, did not lack drama in his absence, as it included Jan Kodes, the Czech, and myself in a semi-final that was more or less Kodes' until I miraculously managed to steal it from him. Kodes was leading 5-1 in the deciding set when the "incredible" happened. 5-1 became 5-2, 5-3, 5-4, 5-5. Then I lost my service but countered swiftly and got tiebreak at 6-6. From there, I went swiftly on to 4-1, missed a match-point at 6-3, but won the next and thus the match with 7-4 in tiebreak.

The final against Tom Okker was settled in the very first set. Okker was leading 5-2, and had five set points, but I managed to come back and win the set by 7-6. After that reverse, Okker seemed very surprised, almost shocked, and never really recovered, so I won both the second and third sets 6-1.

The last tournament in this tour was the American Lawn Tennis Championships, but already before my arrival in New York and Forest Hills, I had a feeling that my journey back to Sweden was not far off. I had quite simply had enough of tennis and progress, and promised myself a lovely six-week holiday after Forest Hills, a promise I fulfilled, as I was knocked out by the Indian, Vijay Amritraj in a match that went to five sets.

Relaxing at home in Södertälje

A strong forehand

30. The move

One October day in 1974, there were more glaring headlines about the fact that my parents and I were to leave Södertälje in Sweden and move to Monte Carlo in Monaco, news which was received with mixed feelings by the Swedish people, i.e. the minority who occupy themselves writing letters to the daily and weekly papers, even directly to me, too, wishing me luck or calling me a tax-fiddler.

Taxes are considerably lower in Monaco than they are in Sweden, but the real reason for my move is this: many of the big tennis tournaments are played in Europe, near to Monte Carlo, and for two years my parents and I had been considering moving. Taking this step on to the continent of Europe would mean that we would be much closer to each other, and I would be able to see my parents very much more often.

Many people think that my financial adviser, Mark McCormack, was behind the move to Monte Carlo, but the fact is I myself took the initiative and made the suggestion shortly after I signed an agreement with him. McCormack promised to work on the matter and try to find a suitable apartment, and I was just as surprised as everyone else when he gave the all-clear in Monaco. It could just as easily have been Italy, Spain, Switzerland or France.

Shortly before the Stockholm Open, I paid a lightning visit to Monte Carlo with my parents to inspect McCormack's "find", and it really did seem that my parents were as pleased as I was with the spacious apartment with a wonderful view of the Mediterranean and a glimpse of Italy to the left. An advantage of Monte Carlo is also the climate, sun every day all the year round and very mild winters.

The Stockholm Open

The 1974 Stockholm Open was to be my last tournament in Sweden before the move, and I was determined to give everything to win and take my revenge for that annoying finals defeat (tie-break in the deciding set) against Tom Gorman, USA, the year before. There was nothing much wrong with my form and perhaps I would have achieved my aim if the Dutchman, Tom Okker, hadn't played "the match of his life" against me in the semi-finals, and if I hadn't been afflicted with a troublesome muscle strain in the quarter-finals against Brian Gottfried, USA. Tom beat me 6-4, 5-7, 7-6 (7-5 in tie-break) and then lost the final against Arthur Ashe, USA, in two straight sets, 2-6, 2-6. I watched the final from the

Serving in the Stockholm Open

Proudly displaying *Svenska Dagbladet's* gold medal

stand and thought: "And I usually beat Ashe quite easily . . .!"

But I was not entirely without acclaim on the finals day. During the prize-giving ceremony, I was called down to the court to receive the *Svenska Dagbladet*'s gold medal for "the greatest sports achievement of the year."

I was the 1974 man of the year in Swedish sport, and I appreciated the distinction. The person presenting the prizes was Lennart Bergelin, the first of the two tennis players ever to receive the medal.

Lennart received it in 1950.

"In those days, there wasn't much competition at the top," said Lennart.

"When there wasn't a Björn Borg," I countered.